Parenting Through Love:
Embracing Parenthood with Resilience

Medical Strategies to Deal with Babe's Health

PAPADIT BASSIA

Copyright © Papadit Bassia 2024
Published by Papadit Bassia
eddieba100@gmail.com

All rights reserved. No part of this publication may be reproduced, stored in a retrieval system, or transmitted in any form by any means, electronic, mechanical, photocopying, recording, or otherwise, without the written permission of the copyright owner.

Disclaimer: The author and publisher disclaim any liability or responsibility for any mistakes or consequences resulting from the use or misuse of the information contained in this book. Readers should be aware that this information should not be used as a substitute for professional medical care.

Editor	CAYLA CLEMT
Proofreader and Editor	SHAANAN LLOYD
Design and layout	EDDIE BASSIA
Cover design	CHRIS KANKU
Printing and binding	
ISBN	978-0-7961-8369-9

Dedication

This book is dedicated to my father, Jean Bassia, and my mother, July Bassia. They hold a special and significant place in my heart. When I had a child, I realised the love, patience, and struggles they faced to make me who I am today.

Table of Contents

DEDICATION

FOREWORD

INTRODUCTION

CHAPTER 1 3

ORIGINS 3

CHAPTER 2 11

THE BEGINNING: 11

MODEST GROWTH AND UNEXPECTED CIRCUMSTANCES 11

CHAPTER 3 29

MISGUIDED VISION: 29

FAMILY PROPHECIES AND TRADITIONS 29

CHAPTER 4 35

CHALLENGES OF PARENTHOOD 35

    Before the baby arrives 35
    Pregnancy, Symptoms, and Cravings 36

CHAPTER 5 40

ESTHER'S WHIMS AND THE ARRIVAL OF CHRISTELLA 40

    Growth and Development 50

CHAPTER 6 55

THE CHALLENGES OF MY LITTLE GIRL CHRISTELLA 55

    Christella's Language Skills 55
    Boundless Energy for Play 56
    Unique Eating Preferences 57
    Learning from Christella's Challenges 58

Supporting Christella 59
Embracing Her Unique Qualities 60

CHAPTER 7 62

FINANCIAL LIMITATIONS 62

CHAPTER 8 79

CHILDREN'S HEALTH 79

Programme Enfance En Sante 80
Childhood Illnesses in Christella 83
Homeopathy, Gemmotherapy, and Treatments for Children 89

CHAPTER 9 95

A BALANCED APPROACH TO HEALING: HOW HOME REMEDIES HELPED MY DAUGHTER CHRISTELLA 95

The Role of Homeopathy 96
Practical Strategies for Administering Medicine 97
A Personal Experience: Christella's Journey 98
Natural Remedies and Their Impact 99
Caring for Christella When She Was Sick 102
Creating a Family Far from Home: The Journey of Christella 105

CHAPTER 10 109

TOWARDS A BRIGHT FUTURE 109

REFERENCES 113

Parenting Through Love:
Embracing Parenthood with Resilience

Medical Strategies to Deal with Babe's Health

Foreword

Today, I have something extraordinary to share with you. Right now, it feels like my life is taking an unimaginable turn. Just a few years ago, all my actions revolved around myself and, to some extent, my parents. My concerns were mostly about my work, studies, what to eat, my hobbies, and church activities. But now, everything has changed since I received this news: I am going to be a dad in a few months.

I was a young guy who thought responsibilities were limited to small activities, and now I have to be responsible not only for one person but two. I'll soon be a dad. It's crazy, isn't it? But you know what? I'm nervous, excited, and a little scared about the future and the responsibility that awaits. This little voice in my head asks, "Are you ready for this?" And honestly, I don't know if anyone is ever truly ready for it. But at the same time, there's this other voice, louder and more confident, saying, "You can do it. You're your father's son. If he did it, so can you."

So, how do I prepare for this giant leap into the unknown? Well, let me tell you, Google has become my best friend. From how to change a diaper to soothing a crying baby, I've looked up everything. I even signed up for childbirth preparation classes with my partner, and believe me, it's both an educational and painful experience.

But it's not just the practical skills I'm working on. I'm also focusing on my personal growth. I want to be a positive role model for my child, so I'm doing my best to be more patient, caring, and present in my daily life. Of course, there are moments of doubt. Times when I wonder if I'll measure up. But you know what? Every parent goes through those moments. It's completely normal. What matters is the love and dedication we put into raising our child.

So even though the path to parenthood is fraught with challenges and obstacles, this young future parent is ready to face the future with determination and resilience. Because, in the end, it's love that guides their steps and lights their way to this new chapter of life. I'm delighted to share my experience with you. Throughout this journey, you'll learn about the events that have defined my new life as a rookie dad. In the meantime, let me share what happened during and after the birth of my little girl.

Introduction

Welcome to my story of fatherhood, adversity, and unconditional love. I invite you to dive into the pages of this book where I share my journey to parenthood, a journey filled with obstacles and challenges yet illuminated by the strength of family love. I was born and raised in a family where contrasts were common, cultures intertwined, and origins were a thread in our identity. But nothing could prepare me for the overwhelming adventure that awaited when I embarked on the path of parenthood.

My story begins in South Africa, a country that is not my homeland, but has become my home, my place of life and experiences. It's where I faced the most significant, most bewildering, yet most rewarding challenges of my life: becoming a parent in a foreign land, far from my family roots. My heart was filled with indescribable love when my little girl was born, but my mind quickly confronted a harsh reality. With limited financial resources, every illness and health concern became overwhelming. I found myself juggling anxiety and uncertainty, desperately seeking solutions to ease my daughter's suffering.

That was when the internet became my most precious ally, a lifeline in the tumultuous ocean of worry. Through forums and medical websites, I sought answers, advice, and remedies to soothe my daughter's ailments and bring back her smile. That's where I discovered the power of midwives' advice, these guardians of ancestral wisdom, who shared their experience and invaluable expertise with me.

Above all, I learned to draw from the resources of my own family to listen to the stories of my mother and grandmother, who had faced the storms of motherhood with courage and determination. Grandma's remedies became our most precious gifts, magical potions concocted with love and dedication to relieve my little girl's pains. Yet every victory over illness was only a temporary respite, as the spectre of uncertainty still loomed over our heads.

When the situation became severe, when my daughter's health was in danger, we rushed to the hospital armed with courage and hope, ready to face the unknown with determination. Through the pages of this book, I wish to share with you the highs and lows of this journey, the lessons learned, and the tears shed, but above all, the unconditional love that guided each of my steps. I firmly believe that our tumultuous story can bring a ray of light into the lives of those who feel lost in the darkness of adversity.

This book is dedicated to all families who have experienced tough times, parents who have found themselves in the face of uncertainty, and those who have seen the strength to keep moving forward, even when the road seemed strewn with obstacles. May my words bring comfort and hope to those who need it most. Welcome to my story of parenthood, resilience, and infinite love.

Part one
History of life that we inherited from our parents.

CHAPTER 1

Origins

I come from a somewhat modern family. My dad has a high level of education and a respectable professional background, while my mom is a villager with limited education who comes from a low-income family. Their marriage story is a bit turbulent, so I'll try to summarise the critical points for you.

Let's return to the Democratic Republic of Congo in the late 1960s and early 1970s. A stylish young man of the time falls in love with a villager who has come to the big city of Kinshasa for the first time, accompanying her uncle's wife to help with childcare in his absence. She also took the opportunity to study. She was a pretty girl with a village look. She lived in the same neighbourhood as a young man named Jean, who had just finished his studies. As soon as he finished, he got a decent job at a bank in town. He earned a good salary, and everything was set for an adventure. At that time, a village girl was considered inferior, uncivilised, and lacking primary knowledge of modern life. The idea of marrying a villager was not acceptable to many city families.

Jean came from a modest, cultured, and politicized family. His father was attached to Belgian culture, the country's coloniser. Every first-born child of a Belgian worker received a free scholarship in the name of his father, and Jean completed his university studies and landed an excellent job at the commercial bank. He was an intellectual, very disciplined, and fond of politics, as his father was one of the engineers who worked in the presidential office. On the other hand, the girl came from a poor family in a distant village in the Bandundu province near the Congo River. She wasn't conventionally pretty, but she had an attractive figure. Her clothes resembled those of a Catholic nun. She didn't speak Lingala well, the language spoken in the city; she only spoke French, the official language, and her native tongue.

One day, as Jean returned from work, he encountered a young girl who was completely different from those around him for the first time. He wondered in his heart where this beautiful creature came from. He approached her to get to know her better. After a little conversation, the girl agreed to meet Jean the following evening. This encounter marked the beginning of a relationship that would eventually lead to marriage.

The lovers spent almost all day together, sharing everything, their passionate love pushing them to do some surprising things to please each other. Then, one day, something happened that would change their lives. The girl was waiting for her boyfriend Jean at the bus stop, her face very sad, troubled in her thoughts. When Jean arrived home after work, he found July with tears in her eyes and wondered what had happened to her. She informed him that she was two months pregnant. Understandably, for Jean, this was an opportunity to prove to July that he was a responsible man, that he loved her, and that he was ready for a long-term relationship. But for July, it was a moment of confusion. Although she loved Jean, she wasn't prepared to announce this news to the Catholic sisters, her first spiritual counsellors, as they would feel deeply humiliated. Additionally, Jean's family was not prepared to accept a villager with little education.

Jean gathered the courage to inform his parents of his intention to marry July. Unfortunately, no one in his family accepted this relationship. The entire family was opposed to it. It became his dilemma: obey his parents or follow his emotions. After much reflection, Jean decided to marry July. This news sparked a conflict that would last for years, with effects that still exist today.

With a good job, he rented a house, and they lived together away from the family. Despite their union, they faced many attacks to discourage Jean from sticking to his decision. But they were determined to live together. After nine months of pregnancy, July gave birth to a beautiful baby boy with blue eyes and a completely bald head a child who represented hope for this new couple. The joy of becoming a father filled Jean's mind and soul. He felt like a bird, blessed with all the blessings of heaven. The child helped him discover his true identity. It was madness: he decided to take his child to work with him twice a week. There, the child received the name

"Papadit," meaning "dad said" in French. Despite the courage, patience, and determination that were the keys to this family's success, something would soon disrupt their future.

One day, there was a big family meeting at Jean's house. The main objective was to figure out how to get rid of this woman (July) from the house. The family decided to make July leave, willingly or by force. That evening, around 5:30 p.m., Jean's younger sisters came to the house and found only the mother and her sleeping baby in bed. They entered forcefully, with threats and insults, grabbed July by the hands, poured petrol over her entire body, and set her on fire. It was a scene reminiscent of a dishonourable film. July screamed, cried, and fought with all her might to extinguish the fire on her body. The sisters fled, locking the door behind them. The neighbours heard July's cries and rushed to her aid. The neighbours and relatives arrived at the scene. They managed to break down the door and get July and the child out. While July was fighting, the child slept, unaware of what was happening to his mother. This reality would be hidden from him until adulthood.

The neighbours transported July to the general hospital. When this news was relayed, Jean's younger sister abandoned all her professional duties to assist July and stay with the child at the hospital. Seriously burned all over her body, there was no hope left for July, as her treating doctor specified. The doctor suggested to the family either to remove July from the hospital or to leave her there until her departure (death) because, according to him, she only had a few days left to live. Jean learned of this medical information and, with July's consent, decided to send her back to her native village. July's concern was to die next to her own family.

On the edge of a boat, Jean and July set off for a distant village in the country. Upon arrival at her family's home, there was a great shock, as other members of July's family wanted to retaliate by treating Jean the same way. But he was saved by July's great love, which convinced her family not to make such a mistake against her husband. Calm returned, and the family regained the mother and her child. Anxiety and despair filled the hearts of July's family members. Every day, July's mother prayed to God for a miracle. "My God, I am your servant, please, my God, save my daughter," a prayer of perseverance and faith.

One day, July's mother returned from the fields with firewood and some vegetables for food. She encountered a strange man, filthy, dressed like a vagabond, with dreadlocks like Rasta men. But his face was clear and clean, as if two different people were in one body. He called her in her mother tongue and said, "Mfuti! Do not cry, because Bati has brought a big fish to eat tonight." The grandmother didn't understand the man's message- it was coded. She replied, "Bati is away; he won't be back today." The man replied, "Go and see, " and left without turning back. The grandmother ignored this message because her mind was troubled by July's situation, as she only had a few days left to live. This man was trying to tell her what would happen to July in a few days.

Two days later, the grandmother was preparing "Chinguage," a kind of food made with cassava root. Busy with her work and July sitting beside her, her mother told her the story of "Ngebouny," a great warrior of the time. It is a legend that our ancestors ask us to show the determination and love of a man who fought and sacrificed his life to retrieve the love of his life, which was confiscated by a powerful, arrogant, and wealthy chief in a distant village. To reclaim his life, he made enormous sacrifices that no ordinary man could resist. It was grace and love for this woman that helped him. The end of the story is that he defeated the chief and rescued not only his wife, but also the other women and girls held captive by this chief.

As soon as July looked up, she saw a flame of fire shining like a star. She approached it from afar, curious to see what this light meant. It only took a few seconds to see the fire before her. She shouted, "Mom, look at this light, it's like a big fire!" But her mother couldn't see anything at all. July kept screaming louder and louder. The fire grew bigger and bigger, approaching July. It threw itself onto July's body, lifting her 6 meters high and dropping her to the ground. July was carrying her little boy on her legs. She fell to the left, and the child to her right, into a water basin for washing hands. With her eyes, the grandmother saw her daughter rising like Superman, then falling to the ground herself, screaming. The whole village was alerted after this event. People came from all sides to see this scene. On the spot, July remained unconscious; the grandmother cried and screamed from all sides; the villagers tried to calm her down to understand what had happened. July was taken to a neighbourhood clinic. After a consultation, the nurse asked the family to see a doctor or a village healer because he didn't understand the situation himself. July's family decided to consult the village healer, but he was not available for three days; he was on duty in neighbouring villages. They kept July at her father's house, unconscious, with her eyes closed; her breathing being the only sign of life.

For the family, hope was lost; July would die no matter what the great healer did. The grandmother and uncle had already begun preparing for the funeral instead of waiting for July's actual death. Fundraising, contributions for the burial, etc., were being collected despite July still being alive. July opened her eyes at 11:00am the next day after this event. There was a group of midwives who spent night and day next to July, praying to God to lessen July's suffering so she could die peacefully, as everyone was convinced of July's inevitable death. These women dispersed, crying out and calling for help. "She's resurrected," they said. This news spread throughout the village and its surroundings. July was miraculously saved. Jean learned the news from villagers who came to sell products in the city. He decided to verify the news by going there himself. He was surprised to see July alive and well despite her body still showing signs of the fire inflicted by her sisters in town. He gathered his courage and decided to marry July with her fire scars. By determining to marry July, admiration from urban authorities and all the families who witnessed this event declared that this gesture was an incomparable act of love. Through this gesture, Jean and July had seven children: four boys and three girls, of which I am the eldest.

Jean's love for his wife, July, determination, and courage are my current life's strengths. My father passed away in 2010, but my mother remains the pillar of the family. She even takes care of her sister-in-law's children, who wanted to kill her over 40 years ago. It's the spirit of forgiveness within her. My mother kept her secrets for over 30 years, and I didn't know why. It's only now that I understand the meaning of her silence. She didn't want to create rebels in the family because no one knows the future. She supported all of us without distinction, like children of the same family. For that, I am proud of my mother; I have grown up, I work. I am the fruit of the sacrifice of two people I adore and will always love. Today, I live with my younger brothers and aunts' children who didn't want my mother.

CHAPTER 2

The beginning:
Modest growth and unexpected circumstances

I discussed this story in my last book, "Poverty Is Not a Disease." I'm sharing it again to explain where I come from and what my future holds. I want to share my life story to see how life and courage are connected. I came to South Africa after many brutal wars in my home country. I stayed here to escape from a conflict I didn't understand and to stay safe from the violence that killed so many innocent people. I grew up in a peaceful place, full of happiness and hope for the future, and attended the best schools. I spent my school years in a Catholic boarding school run by the Kinzambi Brothers, about 530 kilometres from the capital.

The school was in a big forest West of Kikwit. There were forests to the North and South of the Kwilu River. We weren't allowed to swim in the river because it had dangerous animals like crocodiles and hippos. The hippos would come out at night to eat in the villagers' cassava fields near our dorms. The main road was 24 kilometres away, and the area was full of wild animals like jackals and snakes. Leaving the school without a guard who knew the village and forest was very dangerous.

My parents sent me to this school because they wanted me to become a religious brother, which is a big honour in our community. Many families tried to send their firstborn to become a Catholic priest or brother. Since I was the oldest, I was chosen for this path, known as an aspirant or novice. This meant I was being trained to become a Catholic priest or brother. Our training included prayer, education, and the church's teachings. We also did manual work like cleaning and maintenance. Saturdays and Sundays were special days for worship and visiting with others.

You can now see the kind of life we had to follow: this routine shaped my behaviour and even my speaking. I was there from grade one to grade twelve. If you think about it, you'll understand how deeply this experience influenced my life and mind. It wasn't a bad experience; it was a crucial part of my education and learning how to take care of myself. During this time, I learned self-discipline and good manners. I learned to wake up on time, make my bed before leaving my room, eat with my mouth closed, not stay up too late, and read a lot to keep my thirst for knowledge alive. For twelve years, this was my life. Unlike other kids, even my siblings, I didn't get to spend much time with my parents. This was because I was the firstborn and, in a way, my parents' offering to God. This boarding school experience added to my family's education. Everyone in my family looked up to me, treating me almost like a little god. They couldn't say no to me because I was seen as the hope and joy of the family. At that time, everything was going well. My father had an excellent job at a commercial bank, and we didn't lack anything. My father also supported other family members. We practiced African solidarity at home. Before school, my parents would buy uniforms, shoes, and notebooks not just for us but also for the children of our uncles and aunts. My father was very generous and social.

Everyone has bad days, so a wise person should always be prepared. They should manage their time, behaviour, emotions, and decisions wisely because today's choices affect the future. We can't predict tomorrow, but good decisions today lead to positive outcomes later. Let me explain why I say this. 1990, our country faced a major crisis due to a struggling economy and a growing population. The opposition pushed for democracy and lobbied the international community and the current regime. Many events took place, but the most shocking was the widespread looting by poorly paid soldiers trying to make their voices heard. Investors felt humiliated, and food, political, and social insecurity spread. This marked the start of a revolution and the rise of group rebellions, leading to a crisis that continues today. It was the first time I truly understood what a crisis meant. We were shielded from it at home thanks to my family's good management. My father lost his job because he was seen supporting the opposition, but this was kept secret from us. Life seemed normal until one terrible day when we discovered no food. We had to go to bed with only a boiled maize meal and two loaves of bread for five children. I will never forget the shock of that day. We felt like our parents had let us down, and my younger brother rebelled, causing everyone to start yelling. It felt like a rebellion, not in the country this time, but in our home. My mother, who was a midwife, calmed us down. We ate simple porridge and bread, but I couldn't sleep that night.

Let me start with a little story. There was a mother who lived peacefully with her young son. She did everything she could to ensure he got a good education. During tough times, she even sold their belongings to survive. As the boy grew older and realised all his mother had done for him, he developed a deep love for her. She was everything to him. But one day, his mother fell ill, and despite his best efforts, she eventually passed away. The boy was devastated. He saw his future as lost without her, the most important person. He stopped working, eating, and taking care of himself, falling into despair and anger at God, blaming Him for all the world's suffering.

After his mother's funeral, he mistreated himself, his neighbours, and even God, waiting for death to take him too. One day, he met an 82-year-old woman on the road. She said to him, "Look around. Do you think you're the only one with problems? Haven't you seen people die before? What's different about your mother's death? She meant everything to you, but that's no excuse to ruin your life. I'm old and will die soon, too. I wouldn't want my children to suffer and be destroyed because of my death.

Parents want their children to succeed and be happy. Many parents, including me, didn't get an education, but we did everything for our children to get one. It's our pride. In heaven, parents want to see their children happy and say to God, 'I completed my mission. Here is the person I left to carry on.' What you're doing now goes against your mother's wishes. It's a shame for your mother, who suffered for you to become a wise man. She would regret having a child like you. By acting like this, you're dishonouring her memory. If you keep this up, you might die soon, but remember, it's children who bury their parents, not the other way around. We're tired of seeing someone act as foolishly as you."

This message hit the boy deeply. It was the first time someone had scolded him instead of comforting him. He stood up, dusted himself before everyone, and shook his head. He looked at the woman with sadness and left without saying a word. The young man stopped crying, realised his mistakes, and continued his life with a new perspective. What's the lesson from this story? As a citizen of this country, you shouldn't just cry like everyone else. Whether the government notices you or not, you must make yourself known to the authorities. It's your right to criticise the government if things aren't working. In a democracy, you can voice your opinion and demand your rights. But remember, life favours the brave, those who take initiative. When everyone is shouting and looking to the left, join the shout but look to the right. Not everyone who cries out benefits from the protest. Right now, our economy is getting worse. Many people are unemployed, and there's a lot of poverty.

What will happen if we do nothing? If we don't try to improve our education, economy, social services, and health care, we'll stay trapped in a bad situation. It's up to us to take action and change our circumstances.

This summarises my journey: from being unemployed to working as a car guard, attending university, and finally becoming a researcher. This transformation was only possible because I had a big vision for the future. I used all my skills and abilities to change my life and add knowledge. It would have been hard to create anything without understanding all the aspects involved. That's why learning is so important. There are many ways to learn; it just depends on your willingness. One thing that changed my perspective was the time I dedicated to research. I can work for hours without eating or doing anything else. The Internet and the library became my passion. I didn't do all this when I was back in my country. Every day, I learn something new. This is the experience I've gained during my time here. A pastor once said, "You have eyes to see, but you do not see." This means that while many people want to grow and succeed, they fail to see the opportunities right before them. You need to focus on what you need. I've spent my time and energy discovering and learning instead of blaming others. If officials adopt this attitude, it will lead to the full development of people in this country. A renewed mindset, rational behaviour, respect for public property and others, and education are the keys to a better life. A good life isn't just for wealthy people; you can have a good life even if you're poor. The key is controlling and guiding your mind and desires in the right direction.

I've never been discouraged by setbacks because I think about my family and my poor mother. This gives me the courage to work hard. Despite the humiliation, I keep going. I'm not ashamed to work as a guard or in security or any other job to make a living. Determination pushes you forward. When you're determined, you can break through barriers that others can't. That's when a new life begins for you. Be aware of what you can become. Success and failure depend on your actions. Progress and consideration for others will depend on how you use this book.

A Journey of Self-Discovery and Lifelong Bonds

During this time of self-discovery, I developed significant relationships with people who would change the course of my life in terms of education and health. These individuals, who were my clients when I worked as a car guard, became some of the most influential people in my life in a country that is not my own. They gave me more than my family members did: the motivation to move forward, the love of mothers and fathers, unconditional friendship, respect, and consideration, among other things.

When I first arrived in South Africa, I was overwhelmed by the sheer enormity of starting anew in a foreign land. The job market was tough, and I took up work as a car guard, a role many might dismiss as insignificant. However, this very position led me to cross paths with some of the most influential people in my life. At first, my interactions were purely professional. I was there to watch over the vehicles, ensuring their safety while the owners did their business. It was a modest job, but I performed with dedication and integrity. Little did I know that these brief, daily encounters would lay the foundation for relationships that would alter the trajectory of my life.

Arlene: A Mother's Love in a Foreign Land

Arlene, a former lecturer at Cambridge School, was one of the first people to extend a hand of friendship. Arlene saw beyond the surface, recognising potential where others might have seen only a car guard. Her kindness was not just in words but in actions. She took the time to learn about my background, my aspirations, and the challenges I faced. Arlene became more than just a mentor; she became a mother figure to me. She introduced me to educational opportunities, guided me through the complexities of university applications, and provided unwavering support throughout my academic journey. Her sacrifices were immense. She often went out of her way to ensure I had everything I needed, from books to a place to stay during difficult times. In our countless conversations, Arlene shared not only her knowledge but also her life experiences. She taught me the value of perseverance, the importance of education, and the strength found in kindness and empathy. Through her, I learned that family is not just about blood relations but about the connections we forge with those who genuinely care for us.

The Windermere Connection: Charles and Evelyn

Craig and Evelyn Watson, who sadly passed away, were another pair of angels in my life. Meeting them was serendipitous as if fate had intertwined our paths. They introduced me to the path of higher education, opening doors I never thought possible. Craig was a man of vision and generosity. He saw my potential and believed in my ability to achieve great things. He often said that education was the key to unlocking one's full potential, a mantra that resonated deeply with me. With his support, I navigated the unfamiliar territory of university life, tackling challenges with newfound confidence. Evelyn, with her warmth and wisdom, was a guiding light. Her encouragement and faith in my abilities were instrumental in my transformation. She believed in nurturing talents and provided the resources and emotional support needed to succeed. Her passing in 2021 was a profound loss, but her legacy lives on through the countless lives she touched, mine included.

Charis Meyer and Her Family: The Embodiment of Kindness

Charis Meyer and her husband were yet another testament to the kindness of strangers who became family. They showed me the true meaning of family kindness. Their home was always open to me, a sanctuary where I found shelter, love, and acceptance. Charis's family treated me as one of their own. Their young child became like a sibling to me, and their home was a place of warmth and laughter. They taught me the importance of family bonds, the joy of sharing, and the beauty of unconditional support. These experiences were invaluable, especially when I felt lost or overwhelmed.

The Durban North Neighbours Group: A Community of Support

All these remarkable individuals were part of the Durban North Neighbours Group, a community that epitomised the spirit of Ubuntu – "I am because we are." This group was more than just a network; it was a family. The support I received from this community was overwhelming and heartfelt. The Durban North Neighbours Group was a diverse collection of individuals bound by a common goal: to support and uplift one another. Their collective support gave me the strength to persevere through the most challenging times. They were there for me in moments of joy and despair. Their moral support, words of encouragement, and practical assistance were crucial in my journey.

Nick Mavian, Caron Lloyd, and Mother Marie: Pillars of Strength

Among the many Durban North Neighbours Group members, Nick Mavian and Caron Lloyd stood out for their unwavering support. Nick's wisdom and guidance were invaluable, while Caron's compassionate nature provided comfort and reassurance. They were always ready to lend a hand, offering advice and support whenever needed. Mother Marie, another pillar of strength, represented my determination and resilience. She embodied the qualities of a nurturing yet firm figure who pushed me to strive for excellence. Her belief in my potential was a driving force that kept me going, even when the odds seemed insurmountable.

A Journey of Transformation

The journey from being a car guard to a university graduate was not easy. It was fraught with challenges, self-doubt, and moments of despair. However, the support of these incredible individuals made all the difference. They provided not just the resources but also the emotional and moral support needed to overcome obstacles. Education was the cornerstone of this transformation. Through the guidance of mentors like Arlene, Craig, and Evelyn, I pursued higher education and unlocked previously impossible opportunities. Their belief in the power of education inspired me to work hard and persevere, no matter how tough the circumstances.

The Power of Unconditional Friendship

One of the most profound lessons I learned during this time was the power of unconditional friendship. The relationships I formed were not based on transactions or expectations but on genuine care and mutual respect. These friendships were a source of strength and motivation, helping me navigate life's complexities in a foreign land. Unconditional friendship meant being there for each other through thick and thin. It meant celebrating each other's successes and providing support during failures. This camaraderie and solidarity were crucial in building a solid support network that helped me achieve my goals.

Respect and Consideration: The Cornerstones of Relationships

Respect and consideration were the cornerstones of the relationships I built during this time. These values were reflected in how we treated each other, fostering an environment of mutual trust and understanding. Respecting each other's backgrounds, experiences, and perspectives allowed us to form meaningful connections. Consideration was about being mindful of each other's needs and circumstances. It was about offering help without being asked, being empathetic, and understanding the challenges others face. This culture of respect and consideration created a supportive and nurturing environment essential for personal growth and development.

Gratitude and Acknowledgment

The role of the Durban North Neighbours Group in my personal growth cannot be overstated. This community was a lifeline during difficult times, providing material support and a sense of belonging and purpose. The collective strength of this group was a testament to the power of community in fostering resilience and growth. Being part of this community taught me the importance of giving back. The support I received inspired me to help others in similar situations, creating a cycle of kindness and support that benefited everyone involved. This sense of community and mutual support was crucial to my success. Reflecting on this journey, I am immensely grateful to everyone who played a role in my transformation. Their kindness, support, and belief in me were the driving forces behind my success. Acknowledging their contributions is not just a formality but a heartfelt expression of thanks for their profound impact on my life. I can't name the other people because I know them, but we speak almost every weekend. I never dared to ask their names. They also played a significant role in my learning. When others saw me as a poor, worthless car guard, they invested in me. Many thanks again, too.

The Future: Building on a Foundation of Support

As I look to the future, I am determined to build on the foundation of support and kindness that I received. I aim to use my education and experiences to impact my community and beyond positively. The lessons I learned about perseverance, compassion, and the power of community will guide me in my future endeavours. The journey of self-discovery is ongoing, and I am committed to continuing this process with the same spirit of openness and gratitude. The relationships I formed during this time will remain a cornerstone of my life, providing inspiration and support as I navigate new challenges and opportunities.

My graduation in 2023

In conclusion, this journey of self-discovery and transformation was made possible by the extraordinary kindness and support of the individuals I encountered. Their impact on my life is immeasurable, and their contributions have shaped the person I am today. This experience is a testament to the power of human kindness, the importance of community, and the profound impact of unconditional support and friendship. As I move forward, I carry the lessons learned and the relationships forged during this transformative period. These experiences have changed my life and instilled a deep appreciation for the power of kindness and the importance of giving back. The journey continues, and I am excited to see where it will lead, guided by the support and love of those who believed in me from the beginning.

Part Two

The sudden change in destiny is the retreat of your vision and the clarity of what will reach us in the future

CHAPTER 3

Misguided Vision:
Family Prophecies and Traditions

The period of youth is characterised by a basic understanding that allows a person to form their personality, and mental development, and acquire a sense of responsibility in life. It's a stage where everything unfolds in a simple and coordinated manner for some and difficulties and confusion for others. This knowledge comes from the society that surrounds us. Thanks to the magic of new technologies, teenagers gain relational autonomy at an astonishing rate. They form their network of friends, away from their parent's eyes, and assert their individuality.

The vision I developed during my adolescence is as peculiar as my thinking. My grandparents gave me information that would disrupt my perception of things during my childhood. One day, my grandfather called me to help him with his work. While working, he talked to me about our family's genealogy. What's most interesting in this story is that my grandfather's father was a Belgian white man who came to the Congo during colonisation. This explains why there are mixed-race individuals in the family. The funny thing is that my grandparents supposedly predicted my life when I grew up, stating that I must marry a white European woman. This must happen when I am older to preserve tradition. Why only a white woman? This question has not been answered to this day. This little declaration from my grandparents was ingrained in my head like a permanent marker. It became a tune my mother would remind me of, emphasising the importance and responsibility of this declaration and the advantages of obeying grandparents. Eventually, I started to believe in this message. It had preservative effects. Throughout my school and university journey, I only reinforced this thought that one day, I would have a white wife. That's when I began to love cinema and anything related to women, for example, actresses, singers, and athletes.

Since I was little, movies and actresses always had a special place in my heart. Great actresses like Angelina Jolie, with her bold allure. Julia Roberts and her radiant smile, Jennifer Lawrence and her charisma, Natalie Portman and her talent, and French icons like Catherine Deneuve and Sophie Marceau. Sophie Marceau, especially, made me believe in my grandfather's prophecy. She was the epitome of beauty and charm for me. Thanks to her, I started dreaming of a splendid marriage and a life in Europe with beautiful and happy children. Marion Cotillard is also one of the actresses I admire. The beauty of white women fascinated me. Gradually, I became interested in everything related to marriage, with the idea that one day, I would get married, and my wedding would be grand. I dreamed of a magnificent wedding, worthy of the greats of this world, then living in Europe and having beautiful children, with the firstborn being a boy.

I lived in my thoughts like a dreamer. In French, the expression "faire des chateaux en Espagne" means dreaming impossible dreams. For years, I waited as if this dream woman would come looking for me at home. At the university where I studied, I abstained from dating girls to obey my grandparents' wishes. In our family, grandparents are like gods to children. Their ancestors and God bless those who obey their words or follow their instructions. But, surprisingly, my father did not believe in this prophecy. He simply asked me to focus on my studies and forget this story. On the other hand, my mother was the messenger who reminded me daily of my future, as if she were a prophetess. Sometimes, I was considered a separatist and a troublemaker for energetically defending my grandparents' words. My father blamed my grandparents for what he called "brainwashing."

I finished university, years passed, and nothing happened. My grandparents died, and my father, who was ill, was also ready to die. Time was moving on, but where was the prophecy? In my family, grandparents were revered. Their words were commands, and those who followed them were blessed. My grandfather prophesied that I would marry an extraordinary woman and that we would have a wonderful life. However, for my father, the important thing was that I focus on my studies and build a solid career. This difference in vision often created tensions at home. My father accused my grandparents of crippling me with their beliefs.

While at university, I respected my grandparents' wishes and refrained from dating girls. I firmly believed that the woman of my dreams would come to me like magic. But years passed, and nothing happened. I finished my studies and got my diploma, but the prophecy remained unfulfilled. My grandparents passed away, and my father, falling ill, also seemed close to the end. The prophecy seemed to fade away with them.

That's when my father, desperate about my situation, gave me an ultimatum. He said, "If you don't introduce me to a fiancée in six months, I will find a wife for you." This statement shook me. Once so sceptical about prophecies, my father was now ready to take drastic measures to ensure I didn't stay single. Not wanting to accept a wife my father chose, I decided to take matters into my own hands. I met Esther, one of the students at the school where I taught. She was beautiful, intelligent, and kind, everything I could hope for. We started dating, and quickly, our relationship became serious. Esther became the mother of my children, and despite our meeting not precisely matching my grandfather's prophecy, she was everything I had hoped for.

Looking back, I realise that dreams and prophecies have a strange way of manifesting. Sometimes, what we expect doesn't happen in the way we imagined. Life is full of surprises and unexpected turns. Although my grandfather's prophecy didn't come true literally, it guided me throughout my life, giving me a goal and hope. Today, I am happy with Esther and our children.

My father eventually accepted our union, and my mother continued to believe that the prophecy came true. The dreams of grandeur and a sumptuous wedding may have evolved, but they have given way to a reality just as beautiful. With its unpredictability and surprises, life has a charm that even the most beautiful dreams cannot match. Thus, the dreams of castles in Spain taught me to hope and believe in something more significant. And even if these dreams don't always come true as expected, they push us to move forward, search, and eventually find our happiness.

My beautiful wife, Esther.

CHAPTER 4

Challenges of Parenthood

Before the baby arrives

The anticipation of a baby's arrival is often filled with strong emotions and upheavals, both physical and emotional. For my wife, this period was marked by unexpected complications, a rollercoaster of anxiety and fear, sometimes exacerbated by typical pregnancy symptoms.

From the early months, my wife felt increasing anxiety as pregnancy symptoms set in. Relentless morning sickness and chronic fatigue turned her daily life into a real challenge, leaving little room for serenity. Each visit to the doctor was an opportunity for new worries, each ultrasound a surge of anxiety until the soothing sound of our baby's heartbeat reassured us, if only for a moment. But it wasn't just the physical symptoms that tormented my wife. The fear of the unknown, of childbirth, of the responsibility of being a parent, weighed heavily on her already fragile shoulders. Restless nights were the stage for her darkest thoughts and most profound doubts as we navigated the tumultuous waters of impending parenthood together. Sometimes, this anxiety manifested as cravings inexplicable mood swings that seemed to come out of nowhere. Sudden and uncontrollable cravings for strawberries at three in the morning, constant tears over seemingly insignificant things, all manifestations of the emotional rollercoaster my wife was going through daily.

As a man, it was sometimes difficult for me to understand these mood swings, these outbursts of anger or sadness that seemed to come without warning. But over time, I learned to be there for her, to offer her my support and listening ear, even when her emotions seemed irrational or bewildering. Ultimately, despite all the difficulties and tensions that marked this period, the love that binds us was our anchor, our lighthouse in the storm. Every shared moment and embrace strengthened our bond and reminded us that we were on this adventure together, for better or worse.

Pregnancy, Symptoms, and Cravings

Pregnancy is an extraordinary period in a woman's life, but many physical and emotional symptoms also accompany it. From the first weeks, some women may experience characteristic symptoms such as morning sickness and increased fatigue. These symptoms can vary in intensity from one woman to another and sometimes make daily life difficult to manage. In addition to physical symptoms, pregnancy can also be a time of emotional challenges. Fear of the unknown, doubts about one's ability to be a good mother, anxiety about childbirth, and the responsibilities that come with it can weigh heavily on the mind of a pregnant woman. It is entirely normal for expectant mothers to experience a wide range of emotions, from excitement to anxiety, from joy to sadness.

Significant physical and emotional changes mark the stages of pregnancy. During the first trimester, a woman's body undergoes profound transformations to accommodate and nourish the developing foetus. Morning sickness, fatigue, and hormonal changes are often at their peak during this period. The second trimester is frequently described as the most enjoyable pregnancy period, with the disappearance of troublesome symptoms and the return of renewed energy. It is also the time when the baby's first movements can be felt, creating a solid emotional bond between mother and unborn child. The third trimester is marked by the rapid growth of the baby, which can lead to increased physical discomfort for the mother, including back pain, difficulty breathing, and sleep disturbances.

Pregnancy cravings are also a reality for many expectant mothers. Fluctuating hormones can lead to mood swings, sudden cravings, and exaggerated emotional reactions. Partners of pregnant women may sometimes be bewildered by these sudden and unpredictable mood changes. Still, it is essential to remember that these reactions are often temporary and related to the hormonal fluctuations of pregnancy. It is crucial for expectant mothers to feel supported and understood during this time to experience this unique experience as positively as possible. Pregnant women need to receive adequate support from their surroundings, their partner, and their healthcare professionals throughout their pregnancy. The partners of pregnant women can play a crucial role by offering emotional support, helping with household chores, and being present during medical appointments. Health professionals, such as midwives and doctors, can also provide valuable support by answering the questions and concerns of pregnant women, monitoring their health and that of their baby, and providing them with advice and resources to help them navigate through the stages of pregnancy as smoothly as possible.

Finally, pregnant women need to take care of themselves during this time. This includes eating a healthy and balanced diet, engaging in regular exercise suitable for their physical condition, and getting enough rest and relaxation to help reduce stress and promote overall well-being. Every pregnant woman has her journey through pregnancy, with its challenges and triumphs. It's important to remember that each experience is unique, and every woman deserves to be supported and respected in her path to motherhood. Pregnancy offers the opportunity to connect with one's own body in a new and profound way, to develop a unique bond with the unborn baby, and to prepare to embrace the role of parent with all the love and devotion one can offer. Whether it's navigating the highs and lows of pregnancy symptoms, the emotional challenges of impending motherhood, or the sometimes puzzling whims of pregnancy, every moment of this journey is a step toward creating a new life, a life filled with love, happiness, and wonders.

In conclusion, pregnancy is a complex and beautiful experience, full of challenges and rewards. By surrounding themselves with support, taking care of themselves, and embracing each moment with gratitude and determination, pregnant women can navigate this time with confidence and serenity, ready to welcome their babies with all the love and tenderness they have to offer.

CHAPTER 5

Esther's Whims and the Arrival of Christella

Esther's pregnancy had started like a dream, a whisper of happiness and anticipation as we eagerly awaited the arrival of our first child. But as the weeks went by, this dream had turned into a whirlwind of emotions, unpleasant symptoms, and tensions that sometimes threatened our harmony at home.

From the early weeks, Esther had been overwhelmed by typical pregnancy symptoms: morning sickness, extreme fatigue, inexplicable mood swings. These symptoms, though expected, were often more intense and disruptive than she had imagined, leaving her exhausted and emotionally vulnerable. Visiting the doctor brought little comfort, as each new worry or symptom elicited fresh fears and anxieties in Esther. She was terrified of not being up to the task as a mother, of not being able to protect our unborn child from the dangers of the outside world. This anxiety, combined with the hormonal upheavals of pregnancy, had a profound impact on our relationship. Minor disagreements in daily life often took on disproportionate proportions, turning our conversations into unnecessary disputes and conflicts. I struggled to understand Esther's sudden and unpredictable mood swings, sometimes feeling overwhelmed by the force of her emotions.

But it wasn't just the physical and emotional symptoms of pregnancy that caused tensions between us. Pregnancy whims had become a daily reality, with sudden and irresistible cravings, demanding and sometimes bewildering requests. There were moments when I found it challenging to handle Esther's whims, feeling frustrated and helpless in the face of her incessant and sometimes irrational demands. But over time, I had learned to be patient, to listen carefully to her needs, and to offer her my unconditional support, even when it meant giving in to her most extravagant whims.

Despite the tensions and difficulties, we also had moments of tenderness and deep connection. Every ultrasound, every heartbeat of the baby, was an opportunity to celebrate our love and commitment to our growing family. We went through it together, with its ups and downs, joys and challenges. Although sometimes difficult, these moments of struggle have made us stronger as a couple, strengthening our bond and our determination to overcome all obstacles on our path to parenthood.

As the months passed and Esther's pregnancy progressed, the challenges she faced seemed to multiply. Back pain and abdominal cramps became more frequent, preventing her from finding the rest she desperately needed. Restless nights became the norm, with frequent awakenings for trips to the bathroom or simply to find a comfortable position. These sleepless nights were often followed by exhausting days, where Esther struggled to stay awake and focused. Daily tasks that had once been accomplished easily became insurmountable mountains, leaving Esther frustrated and exhausted. This frustration turned into anger, sometimes directed towards me, her husband, who felt powerless in the face of her distress. Our fears and anxieties mingled with our anticipation as the due date approached. We were eager to meet our baby but also anxious about childbirth and the challenges that awaited us as new parents. But we knew we were ready to face these challenges together, united by our love and determination to build a happy and fulfilling family life.

Finally, the pregnancy had been a period of transformation and growth for both of us, filled with challenges and moments of deep connection as we prepared to welcome our baby into our lives. Esther is a woman unlike any other. One strange thing about her is her work ethic. Her concern about going to work and meeting her friends also determined her actions at nine months. A few days before the baby's arrival, Esther decided to go to work. She no longer did anything at home. I became a houseboy, preparing food, doing dishes, cleaning everything, etc. When she returned from work, she phoned me a few minutes before getting out of the taxi on the main road to come pick her up and support her. It became my second job. But the much-awaited day of childbirth had finally arrived. We were ready to face this crucial step, although apprehension and excitement mingled in our minds. Esther was brave and determined as we went to the hospital, prepared to face the challenges of childbirth with strength and resilience. The following hours were intense and exhausting, but thanks to the reassuring presence of the medical team and my constant support, Esther went through each contraction with courage and determination. Finally, after hours of hard work, our baby was born, filling the room with their first cries and our overflowing joy.

When our baby finally arrived, the pain and fear dissipated, giving way to a feeling of pure and indescribable joy. In my wife's arms, I saw the strength and determination that had carried her through the darkest moments, and I knew that we were ready to face the challenges of parenthood hand-in-hand, united by unwavering love. My little girl's arrival was a magical and emotional moment that will forever be etched in my memory. After nine months of anxious waiting and feverish preparations, the long-awaited day finally arrived, illuminating our lives with a new light and unconditional love.

On the morning of her birth, the hospital was filled with an electric atmosphere of anticipation and excitement. Every moment was filled with excitement as we prepared to welcome our precious baby. When the moment finally arrived, the frantic pace of the delivery room suddenly turned into solemn silence, broken only by the beating of my wife's heart and the whispered encouragement of the medical team. In that suspended moment, the whole world seemed to hold its breath, eagerly awaiting the arrival of our little wonder.

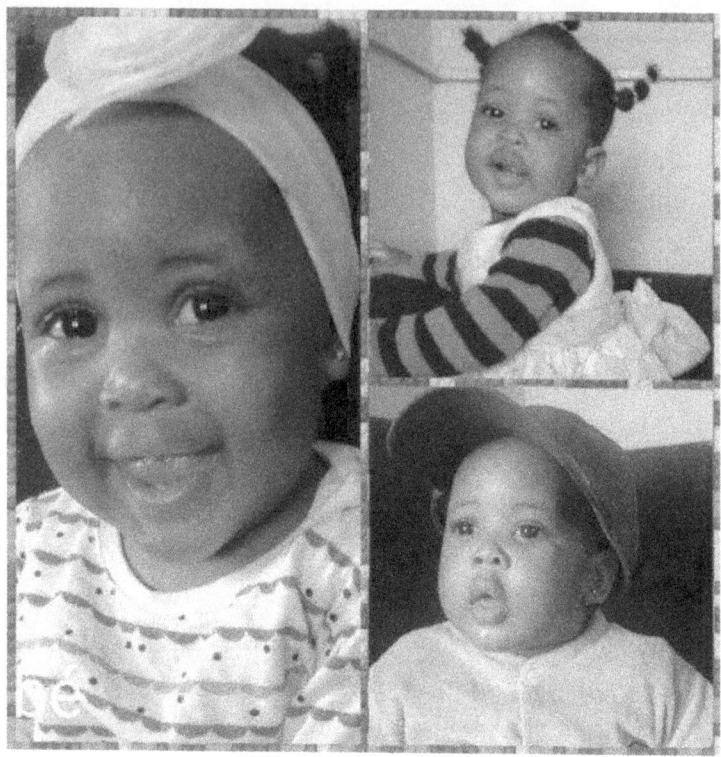

And then, in an instant, everything changed. A loud cry pierced the air, filling the room with life and happiness as our daughter made her entrance into the world. It was a moment of pure magic as I saw her for the first time, her tiny fists clenched, her curious eyes sweeping her new surroundings. It was a moment of pure happiness as we welcomed our daughter into our arms; a little wonder came to enrich our lives with joy and love. Esther radiated happiness as she held our baby against her chest, her eyes shining with tears of joy and exhaustion.

The following hours were filled with indescribable bliss as we rejoiced in the arrival of our daughter. The first moments spent together were like a dream, filled with love as we marvelled at every little detail of her tiny person. Every moment spent with her was a blessing, a constant reminder of the beauty and fragility of life. We were amazed by her perfection and little face that already seemed to reflect her unique personality.

My little girl's arrival transformed our lives profoundly and unforgettably. She brought a new light to our days, an unconditional love that filled our hearts with ineffable joy. She was our little miracle, our ray of sunshine in a sometimes dark and troubled world. And even when the nights were long and exhausting, even when the challenges of parenthood seemed impossible, we were united in our love for her, ready to face any obstacles to protect and cherish our precious little girl. Looking back on this blessed day, I am filled with gratitude and happiness. My daughter's arrival was the most beautiful gift that life has ever given me, and I will continue to cherish every moment I spend with her for the rest of my days.

Every day with my little girl was a new adventure, filled with discoveries and moments of closeness that strengthened our unique bond. The first weeks of her life were a period of mutual discovery as we learned to know and understand each other. The nights were sometimes long and restless, punctuated by cries and frequent awakenings, but even in the most challenging moments, the love I felt for my little girl remained unshakable. I rose each time to meet her needs, knowing that every moment spent with her was precious and irreplaceable. The days were filled with moments of joy and happiness as we explored the world together. My daughter's radiant smiles lit up every room we entered, bringing light and warmth to all who crossed her path.

Over time, we found our rhythm as parents, learning to respond to our baby's needs with confidence and assurance. Our daughter's smiles and coos were a constant source of joy and happiness, reminding us every day of the blessing we had in our lives. Looking back on the first years of her life, I am grateful for every moment I spent with my little girl. Every laugh, hug, and kiss were a precious treasure I will cherish forever in my heart. And as we move forward together into the future, I know that our bond will continue to strengthen and flourish, nourished by the love and tenderness that unites us. My little girl is my greatest gift, my most incredible pride, and I am grateful daily for the chance to be her parent. Every stage of her growth was a new opportunity to celebrate her achievements and encourage her in her challenges. From her first words to her first steps, I witnessed her evolution with indescribable pride, knowing I had the privilege of being there for her every step.

The challenges of parenthood were not lacking, but every obstacle overcome strengthened our bond and our determination to do our best for her. The sleepless nights, the tantrums, the fears, and the doubts; we faced them together, hand-in-hand. My little girl grew into a vibrant and curious young woman with a keen mind and a thirst for discovering the world around her. She amazed me daily with her creativity, intelligence, and compassion for others.

We faced unanticipated challenges during the first few months with our little one. Our baby was difficult to soothe; she seemed to follow her own rhythm, sleeping during the day and waking at night, leaving us with exhausting sleepless nights. Her constant crying seemed to haunt us, leaving us feeling helpless and drained like inexperienced parents desperately seeking answers to our questions. We were faced with a mountain of doubts and uncertainties. Was it hunger, pain, or discomfort? We desperately sought to understand what might be bothering our child, but every attempt seemed to fail. We were overwhelmed by the situation, unable to find a solution to her constant crying. The nights were tough. We took turns trying to calm our baby, but nothing seemed to work. She cried relentlessly, her piercing squeals echoing through the house like a reflection of our helplessness. We were exhausted and on the verge of breaking down, but our love for our baby remained unshakable, giving us the strength to carry on despite it all.

As novice parents, we learned to trust our instincts and support each other through the tough times. We found solace in our love for our child, a powerful force that helped us weather the storms with courage and determination. Eventually, things began to improve. We found a routine that worked for our family, learning to respond to our baby's needs with patience and love. The incessant crying subsided, replaced by shy smiles and moments of closeness that reminded us why we had chosen to be parents. The first months with our baby were also a period of learning and growth for all of us. We got to know our child, understand her needs, and adapt to her changing demands. And while challenges were plentiful, our love for our little one never wavered, guiding us through the dark moments toward the light of infinite love and joy.

Gradually, we found strategies to help our baby calm down and find sleep. We discovered that gentle lullabies and comforting cuddles could soothe her cries and help her drift off peacefully. We also learned to recognise her hunger, fatigue, and discomfort cues, allowing us to meet her needs better and provide the support she desperately needed. Over time, our baby became calmer and more predictable, allowing us to regain a semblance of normalcy in our daily lives. Sleepless nights gradually turned into peaceful nights, and constant crying gave way to moments of happiness and family bonding.

Today, our little one is a ray of sunshine in our lives, filling our home with laughter, cuddles, and joy. We are grateful for the lessons we've learned during these tumultuous first months, as they have helped us become stronger, more attentive, and more loving parents. As we continue our journey as a family, we know that new challenges await us, but we are ready to face them with courage and determination. Our baby is our greatest treasure, and we will do everything possible to offer her a life filled with love, security, and happiness. Every day is a new adventure with our little one, filled with moments of joy and discovery. We've learned to savour each moment, to be grateful for the small miracles of life unfolding before our eyes. We've discovered that even in the most challenging moments, love can be a powerful force that guides and sustains us. Our baby is our greatest gift, a source of infinite joy that illuminates our lives with her radiant light. We look forward to what the future holds in her company, knowing that no matter what challenges come our way, we'll face them together as a family united by love and determination.

Ultimately, the first months of our baby's life have been a growth and transformation for all of us. We've learned about ourselves as parents, discovered the wonders of parenthood, and marvelled at the miracles of life. Looking back on this turbulent period, we are grateful for every precious moment we've shared with our little one. Every smile, every giggle, every gesture remains etched in our memory, a source of comfort and infinite happiness. And now, as we look to the future, we do so with confidence and determination. We know that no matter what life has in store, our love for our baby will always remain as strong and deep, a guiding light in the dark and uncertain times.

Growth and Development

Our baby Christella's growth and development is a journey filled with twists, laughter, and occasional challenges. From the moment she arrived, Christella was determined to explore every corner of her environment, whether it was enthusiastically grabbing small objects or bravely venturing to climb mountains (well, stairs, but you get the idea). From a very young age, Christella showed an affinity for language. Even before uttering her first words, she listened attentively to the stories read to her, absorbing each word with fascination. When she began to speak, she quickly surpassed expectations by uttering "Dada" and "Mama" and forming complete sentences worthy of a linguistic expert. But with language development came the challenge of testing limits. Between two and three years old, Christella decided that rules were more like suggestions rather than strict directives to be followed. Her parents' frequent "no's" was like an invitation to explore the unknown, which sometimes led to some comical situations.

During her pre-school years, Christella continued to develop in all areas. Her boundless imagination led her to explore fantastic worlds populated by imaginary friends and strange creatures. She learned to resolve conflicts with strategies worthy of a budding diplomat while navigating skilfully through the sometimes tumultuous waters of social relationships. And, of course, there were the childhood fears that added a touch of suspense to Christella's adventure. From the "monster in the closet" to mysterious shadows in the night, each fear was a challenge to overcome with bravery (and sometimes with the help of a special blanket or beloved stuffed animal).

As Christella grew, she continued to amaze and delight everyone she encountered. Her cognitive and emotional development was a symphony of curiosity, exploration, and unconditional love. And although the path of growth can be fraught with obstacles, with Christella, each step was a new adventure to overcome. As Christella approached her fourth birthday, her intelligence amazed everyone around her. She increasingly understood the concept of time, even if sometimes everything that had passed was "yesterday" and everything that was going to happen was "tomorrow". Her observations about the world around her were funny and profound, reflecting her growing ability to understand and interpret her environment. When Christella reached age five, she was already a budding philosopher, asking questions about the meaning of life and why the sky is blue. Her vocabulary had expanded by leaps and bounds, understanding thousands of words and forming sentences that impressed even the most erudite adults. But of course, with growth also come emotional challenges. Separations from her parents, whether at bedtime or daycare, were sometimes marked by tears and cries. Fortunately, her faithful stuffed animal was always there to comfort and remind her that she was never alone.

Christella began exploring new social horizons between three and five years old, forming friendships with other children and learning the importance of sharing and cooperation in her games. She discovered the meaning of self through her possessions, proudly asserting, "It's mine!" while still seeking comfort and security from her parents when needed. And despite the childhood fears that occasionally arose, Christella showed courageous determination to face every challenge with a smile. She brightened each day with her sparkling humour and sharp wit for those fortunate to cross her path. Thus, Christella's development until age five was an adventure full of laughter, learning, and unforgettable moments. As she continued to grow and evolve, one thing was for sure: the world would never be big enough to contain all the magic she brought.

As Christella grew, she continued to amaze and delight everyone around her. Approaching her sixth birthday, she had become a fearless little explorer, discovering the world with curiosity and audacity. Her intelligence and quick wit were still present. She absorbed knowledge like a sponge at school and asked questions that sometimes challenged even her most experienced teachers. Her love for learning was contagious, inspiring her classmates to immerse themselves in the wonderful world of discovery. But Christella's development was not limited to intellect alone. Emotionally, she continued to grow and flourish, developing social skills that allowed her to forge strong bonds with those around her. Her natural empathy and ability to understand others' emotions made her a precious friend and invaluable support for those in need. Of course, there were still ups and downs on the growth path. Moments of frustration and disappointment mingled with joys and triumphs, but Christella faced them all with remarkable resilience and unwavering optimism. After all, each challenge was an opportunity to grow and learn, a valuable lesson to take on her journey into the future. As Christella celebrated her fifth birthday, she eagerly looked towards the future, ready to face new challenges, embrace new adventures, and continue to grow and flourish in the world that awaited her. For Christella, the growth journey was an endless adventure filled with promises and infinite possibilities.

Approaching her sixth birthday, Christella was a true whirlwind of energy and creativity. Her boundless imagination led her to adventures as extraordinary as they were fascinating. Whether inventing incredible stories or transforming her room into a magical kingdom, every day was a new opportunity to unleash her overflowing imagination. Her cognitive development continued to progress by leaps and bounds. She astonished her teachers at school with her ability to assimilate new information and solve complex problems. Her sharp mind and thirst for knowledge propelled her to new heights, allowing her to explore new areas of learning with contagious passion. Christella continued to forge strong bonds with her peers on the social front. Her innate sense of empathy and kind-hearted nature made her a precious friend, always ready to lend a hand to those in need. Her circle of friends grew daily, filling her life with laughter, games, and precious memories. Of course, there were always challenges along the way. Moments of doubt and uncertainty mingled with triumphs and successes, but Christella faced them with courage and determination. She knew every obstacle was an opportunity to grow and become more robust, and she was determined to face each challenge with a smile. The first words, the first steps, and every step of her development were a source of pride and joy for me. I watched with wonder and admiration as she grew and flourished before my eyes, becoming more independent and autonomous with each passing day. Our bond grew more intense over the months and years, nourished by the unconditional love and mutual trust that bound us together. My little girl was much more than just a child to me; she was my reason for living, my source of inspiration and daily happiness.

CHAPTER 6

The Challenges of My Little Girl Christella

Christella is a little girl with remarkable qualities. She has an infectious energy, a bright smile, and a heart full of love. However, like every child, she has unique challenges that sometimes make it difficult for others to understand her. As her parent, I've learned to embrace these challenges as part of what makes Christella the particular person she is. Here, I want to share the aspects of her personality that present these challenges, hoping that it can help others understand her better and see the beauty in her uniqueness.

Christella's Language Skills

Christella has always had an impressive command of language for her age. She was articulate and expressive from the time she could talk, often surprising us with her ability to communicate complex ideas and feelings. However, this skill can sometimes be a double-edged sword. While her vocabulary and speech clarity are advanced, she often struggles to moderate her language to match her peers. This can make it hard for other children to relate to her, and she can sometimes come across as overly mature for her age.

Her advanced language skills mean that she sometimes struggles with patience. When she wants something or needs to express herself, she expects others to understand and respond as quickly as she does. This can lead to frustration and misunderstandings with her peers and adults who may not immediately grasp the depth of her thoughts or feelings.

Despite these challenges, Christella's language skills testify to her intelligence and curiosity. She loves to learn new words and uses them with confidence. Encouraging her to be patient and understanding that not everyone communicates at her level has been a learning journey for her and us as her parents. We've worked on teaching her to slow down, listen more, and give others the chance to speak and respond.

Boundless Energy for Play

Christella's energy is boundless. She loves to play and can do so for hours without tiring. This incredible energy is one of her most endearing traits, but it can also be challenging. Unlike many children her age, Christella does not adhere to typical sleep patterns. While other children are winding down for the night, Christella is often just getting started. She can stay awake for hours, full of life and ready to engage in activities that interest her.

Her inability to settle down at night has been a significant challenge. We've tried various bedtime routines and calming techniques, but Christella's body and mind operate on a different clock. This has meant many late nights for our family, often turning into all-nighters that leave us all feeling drained the next day.

Finding ways to help her channel this energy positively has been a continuous process. We encourage outdoor play, physical activities, and even late-night story sessions to help her expend energy. While exhausting, seeing her so full of life and enthusiasm is also a joy. Our goal has been to find a balance that allows her to enjoy her playtime while getting the rest she needs.

Unique Eating Preferences

Another challenge with Christella has been her eating habits. From a young age, she has shown a strong preference for porridge. While other children might explore various foods and enjoy a diverse diet, Christella has remained steadfast in her love for porridge. Getting her to eat anything else is often a battle.

This selective eating has been a concern, as we want to ensure she gets a balanced diet with all the necessary nutrients. We've tried introducing new foods in creative ways, blending vegetables into her porridge, and making mealtime fun and exciting. However, her resistance to change in her diet has remained a consistent hurdle.

It's important that Christella's meals are nutritious, so we've worked closely with her paediatrician to ensure she gets the vitamins and minerals she needs. We've also learned to pick our battles and celebrate small victories when she does try something new. Patience and persistence have been vital, and we continue encouraging her to expand her palate while respecting her preferences.

Learning from Christella's Challenges

Navigating these challenges with Christella has taught us a great deal about patience, understanding, and the importance of seeing the world through her eyes. These aspects that might be seen as weaknesses are also a part of what makes her unique and wonderful. Her advanced language skills, sometimes a source of frustration, are also a gift. They allow her to express herself in ways many children her age cannot. This skill will serve her well as she ages and faces more complex social and academic situations. By helping her learn patience and empathy, we can turn this challenge into a strength. Her boundless energy, while exhausting, is a reflection of her zest for life. Christella approaches each day with enthusiasm and a desire to explore and experience everything around her. Finding ways to channel this energy into positive activities and ensuring she gets enough rest is crucial. We've learned to appreciate her energetic nature and the joy it brings to our lives.

Her selective eating, while challenging, has taught us the importance of perseverance and creativity. We've had to think outside the box to ensure she gets the nutrients, and we've learned to celebrate small victories. This experience has also taught us to respect her preferences and to understand that every child has a unique journey with food.

Supporting Christella

Supporting Christella through these challenges has required patience, creativity, and a lot of love. Here are some strategies that have helped us:

1. Language Skills:

    - Encouraging active listening: We've worked with Christella on the importance of listening to others, taking turns in conversations, and understanding that not everyone communicates at her level.

    - Positive reinforcement: Praising her for using her language skills to help others and showing patience when communicating.

    - Role-playing: Engaging in role-playing activities to help her practice social interactions and improve her patience.

2. Energy Management:

    - Physical activities: Ensuring she has plenty of opportunities to play and expend her energy through outdoor activities and sports.

    - Calming routines: Establishing a calming bedtime routine that includes reading, soft music, and quiet time to help her wind down.

- Flexibility: Being flexible with her schedule and understanding that she may need different sleep patterns than other children.

3. Eating Habits:

- Nutritional supplements: Working with her paediatrician to ensure she gets the necessary nutrients through supplements if needed.

- Creative meals: Incorporating healthy ingredients into her favourite porridge and presenting new foods in fun and exciting ways.

- Patience and persistence: Encouraging her to try new foods without forcing her and celebrating when she does.

Embracing Her Unique Qualities

It's essential to recognise that what might seem like weaknesses are also part of Christella's unique personality and strengths. Her advanced language skills show her intelligence and curiosity. Her boundless energy reflects her zest for life and her desire to explore the world around her. Her selective eating habits highlight her strong will and preferences. By focusing on these strengths and working through the challenges with love and patience, we can help Christella grow into a confident, well-rounded individual. It's about finding the balance between guiding and letting her be herself, understanding her needs, and providing the support she requires to thrive.

As Christella continues to grow, we know there will be more challenges ahead. But with each challenge comes an opportunity for growth, learning, and deeper connection. We are committed to supporting her every step of the way, celebrating her successes, and helping her navigate the difficulties. We look forward to seeing how her language skills develop, how she learns to manage her energy, and how her palate expands. We are excited to witness the person she will become, knowing that her unique qualities make her truly special.

Christella's challenges are part of what makes her who she is. Through her advanced language skills, boundless energy, and unique eating habits, Christella shows us the beauty of individuality. She teaches us to see the world through her eyes and to appreciate the qualities that make each person unique. As parents, our journey with Christella is filled with learning and growth. We are grateful for the opportunity to be part of her life and to help her navigate the challenges she faces. With love, patience, and understanding, we will continue to support her every step of the way, celebrating her unique qualities and helping her thrive in all areas of her life.

CHAPTER 7

Financial Limitations

As new parents, our greatest challenge was undoubtedly posed by limited financial resources. As immigrants in a foreign country, our financial situation was precarious, with every additional expense weighing heavily on our already burdened shoulders. Every dollar spent was a careful calculation; every cent counted with care. We had already juggled the costs of daily life, managing rent, bills, and grocery expenses. But when my daughter fell ill, our fragile financial balance was put to the test. The exorbitant medical costs added to our worries, creating a heart-breaking dilemma.

On one hand, there was the imperative to take care of our child, to ensure her the best possible medical care. But on the other hand, there was the stark reality of our limited finances. Should we deprive ourselves of essentials to pay exorbitant medical fees, jeopardizing our long-term financial security? Or should we seek less expensive alternatives, knowing it could compromise the quality of care for our daughter? The decision was agonizing; each option came with sacrifices and undesirable consequences. We weighed the pros and cons and evaluated all possibilities, but none offered a perfect solution. We consulted friends and family members and sought advice from healthcare professionals, but the answer remained elusive.

Eventually, we had to make a decision, however difficult it was. We opted for a middle-ground solution, seeking ways to reduce costs without severely compromising our daughter's medical care quality. We conducted thorough research, explored all available options, and eventually found a clinic offering affordable services without sacrificing quality. It wasn't a perfect solution by any means. We had to make compromises adjust our expectations, but overall, we chose the best path possible in challenging circumstances. We learned to juggle financial hurdles while ensuring the well-being of our child, navigating with courage and determination through life's storms.

Ultimately, this experience taught us a valuable lesson about resilience, ingenuity, and the strength of parental love. We found creative solutions to complex problems and emerged stronger and more united. And although our path was strewn with obstacles, we traversed each trial with the certainty that love and determination can overcome all hurdles.

In the weeks following the difficult decision we made, we faced a myriad of complex emotions. Guilt gnawed at us, wondering if we had made the right choice for our beloved daughter. Worries about her health and well-being plagued us day and night, creating a crushing weight on our already tired shoulders. Yet, despite the challenges we faced, we found comfort in our family unity. We rallied together, supporting each other at every step of the way. No matter how difficult, every decision was made together in a spirit of collaboration and solidarity. Our love for our daughter was a guiding thread that bound us, giving us the strength to endure even the darkest moments.

In the face of the situation's urgency, I plunged into an ocean of uncertainty and anxiety. My daughter, my most precious treasure, was afflicted by an illness whose symptoms seemed to defy explanation. Every day, I watched her suffer, feeling powerless in the face of her pain, desperate to find a way to alleviate her suffering. It was in these moments of despair that I realised we needed to find alternative solutions to help my daughter regain her health. Conventional medicine offered little hope, and we needed to seek answers to our pressing questions elsewhere. That's when I began to explore the internet in search of answers, advice, and remedies that could assist us in our battle against the illness. Through parent forums and medical websites, I found a sense of camaraderie and solidarity that helped me through the most challenging times. Each shared story, each word of encouragement, was like a soothing balm for my troubled soul. At the same time, I consulted reputable medical sites, seeking reliable, evidence-based information to guide my decisions. I read clinical studies, research reviews, and medical reports, absorbing every morsel of knowledge that could help us in our fight against the illness.

I discovered a treasure trove of knowledge and shared experiences. Touching stories of families facing similar challenges to ours, practical advice on managing symptoms, inspiring testimonials of healing— all of this became our guide in the darkest moments. I delved into reading every article, every testimony, every medical study I could find. Every word was a ray of light in the darkness, a glimmer of hope in an ocean of despair. I noted every detail, every suggestion, every lead that seemed promising, determined to do everything in my power to alleviate the suffering of my beloved daughter. As I delved deeper into my research, I realised that the key to helping my daughter lay in a holistic approach to health. It wasn't just about treating the symptoms of her illness but also strengthening her body, mind, and soul so she could fight the disease with all her might.

So, I began to explore a multitude of alternative treatment options, ranging from acupuncture to meditation to homeopathy and specific diets. Each method was carefully evaluated, weighed against available evidence, and discussed with competent healthcare professionals. Of course, there were moments of doubt and uncertainty. Times when I wondered if I was on the right path and if I was doing everything I could to help my daughter regain her health. But each time, I remembered my daughter's face, strength, and resilience, and I knew I had to keep fighting for her, no matter what obstacles lay in our path.

Every day, I woke up with new hope and a renewed determination to find solutions to alleviate my daughter's illnesses. I devoted endless hours to researching information, consulting experts, and exploring every possible avenue to improve her health. Acupuncture became one of the avenues we explored to relieve my daughter's ailments. I made appointments with an experienced practitioner, hoping this ancient form of Chinese medicine could offer relief where conventional medicine failed. The acupuncture sessions were soothing and relaxing, providing a welcome respite for my daughter and a sense of hope. In parallel, we also adopted a holistic approach to health, focusing on my daughter's diet and lifestyle. We consulted nutritionists and alternative medicine specialists, seeking advice on foods and supplements that could strengthen her immune system and promote healing. The dietary changes were gradual but significant, giving my daughter a new lease on life and energy. Meditation also became an integral part of our daily routine. We practiced relaxation and deep breathing techniques to help my daughter manage the stress and anxiety associated with her illness, and these moments of calm and reflection brought us a sense of inner peace, helping us stay strong and centred in the most challenging times. Over time, our efforts began to bear fruit. My daughter's symptoms eased, her health improved, and a sense of relief and gratitude filled our hearts. We realised that even in the darkest moments, there was always hope, always a possibility of healing and recovery.

Today, my daughter is healthier than ever. She radiates vitality and zest for life. Although our journey has been long and difficult, I know that every challenge we have overcome has made us stronger, more united, and more grateful than ever for the wonders of life and the strength of the human spirit. In our quest for solutions to alleviate our beloved daughter's ailments, we found invaluable support from experienced midwives. Their deep knowledge and gentle, compassionate approach were a lifeline in the darkest moments of our journey.

From the moment we stepped through the doors of the midwife's clinic, we were greeted with warmth and empathy. The experienced midwives took the time to listen to us carefully and understand our concerns and needs before offering solutions tailored to our unique situation. Their wise counsel was infused with ancient wisdom passed down through generations. Their holistic approach to health allowed us to see our daughter not only as a collection of symptoms to treat but as a complex and unique being with her own needs and desires. Each session with the experienced midwives was a lesson in life itself. They shared their expertise, teaching us traditional healing and pain relief techniques. Their skilled hands could find tension points and release them with impressive skill, bringing immediate relief to our suffering daughter. But more than their technical skills, their loving and attentive presence touched us to the core of our being. They were there for us every step of the way, offering unwavering support and a shoulder to lean on when things seemed darkest. Their gentle and compassionate approach transformed our experience of parenthood. Instead of feeling alone and overwhelmed by the challenges of raising our child, we felt supported and encouraged every step of the way. Their reassuring presence allowed us to face the ups and downs of parenthood with more confidence and determination.

Together, we explored many treatment options, from natural remedies to relaxation techniques to advice on diet and lifestyle. Every piece of advice was valuable; every suggestion was taken seriously and respectfully. And over time, we saw significant progress in our daughter's health and well-being. Her symptoms eased and her vitality strengthened. We are deeply grateful for the invaluable support we received from experienced midwives. Their expertise and compassion have been a precious gift in our journey of parenthood, helping us navigate the challenges of family life with grace and resilience.

Today, our daughter is healthier than ever, and we know this would not have been possible without the precious assistance of experienced midwives. Their legacy of wisdom and compassion will continue to guide us in the years to come, reminding us constantly of the power of love and support in life's most challenging moments. Experienced midwives have become much more than just healthcare professionals to us. They have become mentors, guides, and even cherished friends. Their comforting presence has been a source of strength and inspiration, helping us overcome obstacles. Every session with experienced midwives was an opportunity to learn and grow. They shared their vast experience and accumulated wisdom over the years, offering practical advice and much-needed encouragement. Their comforting words and thoughtful gestures made us feel like we were in good hands, even in the most uncertain times. Their holistic approach to health allowed us to see our daughter in a new light. They encouraged us to consider all aspects of her well-being, including her emotional and spiritual state. Their deep understanding of the connection between body, mind, and soul helped us adopt a more comprehensive approach to healing and recovery.

In addition to their medical advice, experienced midwives also guided us emotionally. They helped us navigate the rollercoaster of emotions that often accompany parenthood, offering a sympathetic ear and words of comfort when we needed them most. Their unconditional support gave us the strength to remain strong, even when everything seemed dark around us. We have experienced moments of joy and sorrow, triumph and defeat. But through it all, experienced midwives have remained by our side, guiding us with wisdom and compassion through the ups and downs of family life.

Today, we look back with gratitude on our journey with experienced midwives. Their invaluable support has been a precious gift in our journey of parenthood, helping us raise our daughter with love, compassion, and dedication. We know that the teachings and advice of experienced midwives will continue to guide us in the future. Their legacy of compassion and wisdom will live on in us, constantly reminding us of the importance of kindness and support in family life. In short, experienced midwives have been a light in the darkness, a source of strength and support when we needed it most. Their loving and caring presence will forever be engraved in our hearts, reminding us of the transformative power of love and compassion in family life. Despite our tireless efforts to find alternative solutions, resorting to professional medical care sometimes became inevitable. Hospital visits became an unavoidable reality, reserved for the most severe situations when our home remedies were no longer sufficient to alleviate my daughter's distress. Yet even then, we had to juggle with the high costs of medical care and the limited resources at our disposal.

Each time we stepped through the hospital doors, it was filled with hope and apprehension. We hoped to find answers to our pressing questions, but we also dreaded the financial costs that could result from each visit. For a family with limited resources, every medical expense represented a crushing financial burden, a source of additional stress and anxiety in an already difficult time. However, despite our economic concerns, we knew that our daughter's health and well-being came first. We were willing to do whatever it took to ensure she received the best possible care, even if it meant sacrificing our needs and desires. It was a harsh lesson to learn, but one we were willing to accept for the sake of our beloved child. Hospital visits were often exhausting, both emotionally and financially. We immersed ourselves in a world of medical examinations, costly treatments, and exorbitant medical bills. Each consultation, each test, and each therapy seemed to add up, adding additional pressure to our already burdened shoulders.

Yet, despite the challenges, we found comfort in the support and care provided by the medical staff. Their expertise and compassion brought much-needed relief in the darkest moments of our medical journey. Their dedication to providing quality care to every patient, regardless of their financial status, was a source of inspiration and hope for us all. But even with the medical staff's support, the high medical care costs were often overwhelming. We juggled with medical bills, trying to find ways to pay them while ensuring the essential needs of our family. Sometimes, this meant making difficult choices and sacrificing certain things to ensure our daughter's care. However, despite the financial challenges, we were determined to do everything we could to ensure the health and well-being of our daughter. We sought financial assistance programs, grants, and relief funds to alleviate the financial burden weighing on our shoulders. Every little help was a step closer to saving our beloved daughter, and we were willing to do whatever it took.

In the end, the high costs of medical care were a harsh reminder of the fragility of life and the importance of health. They were also a testament to the need for a more equitable and accessible healthcare system. We hoped to one day live in a world where no one would be forced to choose between their health and their finances, where every individual would have access to the medical care they need when they need it, without worrying about the associated financial costs.

Despite the difficulties and challenges, we overcame this difficult period with courage and determination. We did everything in our power to ensure the best possible care for our daughter, even when costs were high, and resources were limited. And today, as we look back on our journey, we know that every sacrifice was worth it, as we succeeded in protecting and saving the life of our beloved child. We faced difficult choices agonizing decisions about the best way to ensure the medical care our daughter desperately needed. Sometimes, it meant going further into debt, relying on loans or grants to cover medical expenses. Other times, it meant compromising different aspects of our lives, cutting back on expenses to allocate more money to healthcare. The financial burden of medical care was especially heavy as we were already struggling to make ends meet. As immigrants in a foreign country, we had limited financial resources, and every penny counted. Every unexpected expense was a blow to our already tight budget, a harsh reminder of the fragility of our economic situation.

Yet, we were determined not to let financial constraints prevent us from providing the best possible care for our daughter. We were willing to make sacrifices, grit our teeth, and face challenges with courage and determination. For us, the health and well-being of our children were more important than anything else, and we were willing to do whatever it took to preserve them. We sought creative ways to reduce the costs of medical care, exploring options such as financial assistance programs, discounts for low-income patients, and instalment payment plans. Every little saving was a victory, a step closer to the healing of our beloved daughter.

But despite our efforts, medical bills continued to pile up, adding an extra weight to our already heavily burdened shoulders. We juggled payments, trying to balance our medical needs and financial obligations. Sometimes, it meant having to postpone other vital expenses, such as education or housing, to be able to pay medical bills on time. Financial difficulties also took a toll on our mental and emotional health. We found ourselves overwhelmed by stress and anxiety, paralyzed by the fear of not being able to meet our family's needs. Every unpaid medical bill was a harsh reminder of our financial vulnerability, a reminder that we were at the mercy of the high costs of medical care.

Over time, we found ways to cope with our precarious financial situation. We learned to be more frugal and to seek ways to save every penny where possible. Dining out and impulse purchases became luxuries we could no longer afford, sacrificed for our child's health and well-being. Yet, despite the privations and sacrifices, there was a glimmer of hope in our daily lives. Despite her illness, our daughter radiated with joy and energy, reminding us every day of the actual value of life. Her bright smile was our reward, giving us the strength to keep fighting even when obstacles seemed insurmountable. And then, little by little, things began to improve. Our daughter's health improved, allowing us to breathe a little easier. The medical bills gradually dissipated, lightening the financial burden that weighed on our shoulders. We began to glimpse a future where tough times would be behind us, replaced by days of happiness and prosperity.

However, we found comfort in our determination to overcome obstacles together. We drew upon our love and mutual support to give us the strength to keep moving forward, even when times were tough. We learned to be resilient, to find creative solutions to financial problems, and to remain united in adversity. And today, as we look back on our journey, we are proud of our path together. We have faced unimaginable trials, overcome seemingly insurmountable obstacles and weathered financial challenges that could have broken our spirit. But through our determination, resilience, and unconditional love for our daughter, we managed to get through this challenging time and ensure her the best possible care. And for that, we will be eternally grateful. We faced new challenges and trials daily, but we refused to give up. We were determined to do everything to ensure our daughter's well-being, even if it meant overcoming countless financial obstacles. Medical bills were not just pieces of paper; they represented our hopes, fears, dreams, and realities. Every figure written on those pages was a statement of our struggle, evidence of our determination to save our beloved child.

Yet, no matter the obstacle, we found comfort in the support and love of our family and friends. Their loving presence and constant encouragement gave us the strength to fight, even when times were darkest. They were our lifeline in a sea of difficulties, reminding us that we were not alone in this struggle. We also found comfort in the joy and happiness that brightened our days. Our daughter's smiles and contagious laughter were constant reminders of the beauty and magic of life, even in the most challenging times. They were sources of light in the darkness, rays of hope in the storms.

Together, we overcame obstacles that seemed impossible. We faced adversity with courage and determination, refusing to succumb to fear and despair. We were a team united in our determination to protect and save our beloved daughter. And finally, after months of struggle and sacrifice, our efforts paid off. Our daughter began to show signs of healing, recovery, and return to health. Every smile, every laugh, every step towards recovery was a victory, an affirmation of our determination never to give up, even when times were darkest. Today, our daughter is healthier, stronger, and more resilient than ever. She has overcome incredible challenges and shown strength and courage, inspiring and moving us. She is our hero, our source of pride and joy, and we are infinitely grateful to have had the chance to accompany her on her journey to healing.

Today, as we look back on this tumultuous period of our lives, we are filled with gratitude for the lessons we have learned, the obstacles we have overcome, and above all, the unconditional love that has guided us through the darkest moments. We have learned that even in the worst times, there is always light on the horizon, and as long as we remain united as a family, there is nothing we cannot overcome. This trial has also taught us to be grateful for the little things in life. Every moment spent together, every shared burst of laughter, every moment of happiness was a blessing not to be taken for granted. We have learned to savour each moment, appreciate life's simple joys, and be aware that true wealth lies in the bonds we share as a family. Over time, we have also developed greater resilience in adversity. We have learned to adapt to unexpected challenges to find creative solutions to problems in our path. Each obstacle allowed us to grow, strengthen ourselves, and become stronger together.

Although difficulties and sacrifices marked this period of our lives, it was also illuminated by the love and compassion emanating from each family member. We found comfort in our unity, in knowing that we were together, hand in hand, ready to face whatever challenges came our way. Today, our daughter has recovered, healthier than ever. The dark clouds that once hung over us have dissipated, giving way to a clear, bright blue sky. This experience has transformed us and shaped us as a family. We have learned that even in the darkest moments, there is always a glimmer of hope shining in the distance. And as long as we stay together, united in our love and determination, there is nothing we cannot overcome.

Part Three

There is always a way out of the challenges and uncertainty imposed by patients and health,

CHAPTER 8

Children's Health

As I explained previously, Christella was often sick, and we needed to find a permanent solution for her health. My wife and I tried everything, but nothing worked. Her health wasn't improving at all. New symptoms of different illnesses would appear one after another. So, what could we do? This marked the beginning of an intense research journey. After trying everything, we had to apply what we learned to our little girl. We became amateur doctors at home. Here's how we proceeded with her treatment:

Firstly, we stopped all the medications she had been prescribed or that we bought from the pharmacy. We only gave her the medicines specifically recommended by the doctor. Secondly, we decided to use home remedies. We followed midwives' advice, gathered information from the internet, and joined a French program called "Le Programme Enfance En Sante", guided by Madame Anne-Laure Wright, the founder of the organization "Naturelle Maman." Through this program, I learned how to treat children with natural medicine. This program offers a revolutionary approach to caring for children using reliable and safe natural therapies. They provide practical solutions for treating common childhood illnesses such as colds, ear infections, eczema, allergies, and sleep or dietary disorders.

Programme Enfance En Sante

Children often have colds, recurrent ear infections, eczema, allergies, and sleep or dietary disorders. These conditions can affect their well-being and quality of life. Comprehensive approach also aims to help parents strengthen their children's immunity and promote overall family health. By learning to care for their children naturally, parents can offer practical solutions against these conditions and improve the quality of life for the entire family. I found a health program in France called "Maman Naturelle." This organization changed the life of my little girl, Christella. Here are some common diseases in children aged zero to five, along with causes, effects, and treatments using home remedies recommended by the program.

Diversity of therapies:

The program offers a diverse approach to natural treatments. From herbal medicine to homeopathy, aromatherapy, and many others. They give parents the tools to care for their children holistically. There is importance of emotional and psychological support for children; Beyond physical treatments, this program also emphasizes the importance of emotional and psychological support. It firmly believes that addressing these aspects is essential for fostering the overall well-being of children and their families.

Benefits of natural remedies:

Natural therapies offer many benefits, including their effectiveness against various daily ailments and their ability to strengthen immunity naturally. By opting for these solutions, parents can provide their children with effective and safe care.

Differences in children's health:

Recognising differences in children's health is essential. Some are more robust than others and seem less prone to illnesses, while others may be more sensitive and receptive to various ailments. By understanding these differences, parents can better adapt their care strategies to meet the individual needs of their children.

Solutions offered by the program:

The program provides various solutions, including homeopathy, gemmotherapy, and other natural remedies to treat various common ailments in children. By giving these alternative options, the program aims to offer parents effective and safe ways to care for their children's health.

Safety and effectiveness of natural remedies:

Homeopathic remedies, macerates, and other plant extracts are commonly prescribed, with impressive results. For example, Ravintsara, an essential oil with powerful antiviral properties, can be a faithful ally in fighting infections. Its use is safe from age three, and numerous scientific studies prove its effectiveness. It is essential to emphasise that while natural remedies can be effective, their use requires appropriate knowledge and professional guidance. To ensure the safety and effectiveness of treatments, it is recommended that trusted professionals be consulted to use these alternative methods correctly.

Children division:

The program is for those who enjoy robust health and those who are more fragile and prone to common illnesses. The program offers practical solutions to protect children from viruses and strengthen their immune systems. With their four-pillar approach, you can go months without flu, colds, sore throats, or gastroenteritis. You will learn to ensure strong immunity for your children, fully enjoy your family life, and avoid common illnesses.

Example of treatments in Switzerland:

A more natural and homeopathic approach to childhood illnesses is preferred in Switzerland. Parents are more likely to be offered natural treatments in pharmacies, demonstrating these alternative methods' effectiveness in managing children's health.

Their program offers a comprehensive approach to improving your children's health yearly. With simple and easy-to-implement advice, you can build your natural pharmacy and safely care for your children daily. The program provides a valuable opportunity for parents to take charge of their children's health naturally and effectively. By joining the program, parents can benefit from proven advice and solutions and promise a healthier and happier family life through natural treatments. Programs are available worldwide. You can find an association or non-profit organization providing children's health information near you.

Childhood Illnesses in Christella

These are a few of the illnesses Christella faced, with causes and homeopathic treatments provided.

Diarrhoea:

- Symptoms: Liquid or loose stools, abdominal pain, cramps, nausea, dehydration.
- Causes: Viral or bacterial infections, reactions to certain foods or medications, intestinal irritation.
- Treatments: Hydration, healthier diet, monitoring signs of dehydration.

Middle Ear Infection (Otitis Media):

- Symptoms: Ear pain, pressure sensation, hearing difficulties, fever, irritability.
- Causes: Bacterial or viral infection, allergies, nasal congestion, exposure to cigarette smoke.
- Treatments: Warm or cold compresses, pain relievers, elevating head during sleep.

Conjunctivitis:

- Symptoms: Red, irritated, watery eyes, itching, crusts on eyelids, purulent discharge.
- Causes: Viral or bacterial infections, allergies, exposure to irritants, tear duct blockage.
- Treatments: Gently cleaning eyes with warm water, applying warm compresses, avoiding rubbing eyes.

Atopic Dermatitis (Eczema):

- Symptoms: Dry, red, irritated, scaly skin, itching, crusts, fissures.
- Causes: Genetic factors, allergies, dry skin, irritants.

Treatments: Moisturizing with emollient creams, avoiding known triggers, wearing soft cotton clothing.

Cough in Children:

- Causes: Respiratory infections, allergies, asthma, irritants, GERD.
- Symptoms: Dry or productive cough, runny nose, fever, wheezing, phlegm.
- Treatments: Hydration, air humidification, honey, medical consultation.

Constipation in Children:

- Causes: Lack of Fibre, dehydration, eating habit changes, lack of physical activity.
- Symptoms: Difficult or infrequent bowel movements, abdominal pain, discomfort during defecation.
- Treatments: Increase Fibre intake, increase fluid intake, gentle belly massage, physical activity encouragement.

Infant Colic:

- Causes: Digestive immaturity, food sensitivity, intestinal gas.
- Symptoms: Excessive and prolonged crying, usually in the late afternoon or evening.
- Treatments: Gentle belly massage, heat application, frequent feedings.

Colds in Children:

- Causes: Exposure to viruses, developing immune system, contact with other children.
- Symptoms: Runny nose, fever, headaches, fatigue, cough, sore throat.
- Treatments: Hydration, rest, air humidification, relief of congestion.

Fever in Children:

- Causes: Viral or bacterial infections, immune response, vaccinations.
- Symptoms: Elevated body temperature above 38°C (100.4°F), typically associated with illness.
- Treatments: Hydration, rest, lightweight clothing, lukewarm baths, medical consultation.

Teething in Children:

- Causes: Tooth growth, pressure on gums.
- Symptoms: Pain or discomfort in gums, excessive drooling, swollen gums, irritability
- Treatments: Gum massage, teething rings, teething gel, cold foods.

Flu in Children:

- Symptoms: Fever, headaches, fatigue, cough, sore throat, muscle and body aches.
- Causes: Influenza virus, transmission through contact or respiratory droplets, developing immune system.
- Treatments: Rest, hydration, fever reduction, symptom relief, balanced diet, medical consultation.

Sore Throat in Children:

- Symptoms: Sore throat, difficulty swallowing, swollen glands, fever, headache, abdominal pain.
- Causes: Viral or bacterial infections, irritations, tonsillitis, acid reflux.
- Treatments: Drinking warm liquids, gargling, hydration, rest, pain medications, medical consultation.

Excessive Crying in Children:

- Symptoms: Persistent crying, irritability, difficulty sleeping, arching back, clenched fists, flushed face.
- Causes: Hunger, discomfort, fatigue, pain, overstimulation, separation anxiety, need for attention.

- Treatments: Comfort and contact, identifying needs, regular routine, calming environment, medical consultation.

Ear Pain in Children:

- Symptoms: Ear pain, irritability, difficulty sleeping, tugging or pulling at ears, fever.
- Causes: Middle ear infections, external ear infections, barotrauma, foreign body, wisdom teeth.
- Treatments: Warm compresses, ear drops, pain medications, rest, medical consultation.

Gastroenteritis in Children:

- Symptoms: Vomiting, diarrhoea, abdominal pain, fever, dehydration, lethargy.
- Causes: Viruses, bacteria, parasites, toxins, allergic reactions.
- Treatments: Rehydration, light diet, antidiarrheal medications, rest, medical consultation.

Head Trauma in Children:

- Symptoms: Headache, dizziness, nausea, vomiting, loss of consciousness, confusion, irritability.
- Causes: Falls, traffic accidents, sports injuries, physical abuse, domestic accidents.
- Treatments: Medical evaluation, rest and observation, ice application, pain medication, medical follow-up.

Homeopathy, Gemmotherapy, and Treatments for Children

Homeopathy

Homeopathy is a natural medicine that uses highly diluted substances to trigger the body's self-healing mechanisms. Developed in the late 18th century by Samuel Hahnemann, it is based on two main principles: "like cures like" and "law of minimum dose." The idea is that substances that cause symptoms in a healthy person can, in minute amounts, treat similar symptoms in a sick person. Homeopathy is generally considered safe for children because the remedies are highly diluted, minimising the risk of side effects. However, it's essential to consult a healthcare professional before starting any treatment.

Examples of Homeopathic Treatments for Children:

1. Chamomilla: Often used for teething pain and irritability. It can help soothe a restless child who is crying and inconsolable.

2. Arnica Montana: Used for bruises, bumps, and physical trauma. It helps reduce pain and swelling.

3. Belladonna: Employed for high fever with sudden onset. It's useful when the child is flushed, hot, or has a throbbing headache.

Homeopathy is generally considered safe for children because the remedies are highly diluted, minimizing the risk of side effects. However, it's essential to consult a healthcare professional before starting any treatment.

Gemmotherapy

Gemmotherapy is a branch of phytotherapy that uses extracts from plants and trees' buds and young shoots. These embryonic tissues are rich in growth factors and enzymes, making them potent sources of active compounds. Developed by Doctor Pol Henry in the 1950s, gemmotherapy is believed to stimulate the body's detoxification and regenerative processes.

Examples of Gemmotherapy Treatments for Children:

1. Ribes Nigrum (Blackcurrant): Known as a natural anti-inflammatory and immune booster, it treats allergies, asthma, and recurrent infections in children.

2. Corylus Avellana (Hazel): Utilized for respiratory issues, it can help children suffering from bronchitis and other lung-related conditions.

3. Rosa Canina (Wild Rose): Employed to strengthen the immune system, it is handy for preventing frequent colds and flu in children.

Gemmotherapy is valued for its gentle and holistic approach, making it suitable for children. It supports the body's natural healing processes without harsh chemicals.

Practical Applications and Considerations

Both homeopathy and gemmotherapy offer natural alternatives to conventional medicine, especially for children, due to their gentle and non-toxic nature. When using these treatments, it's important to follow a few guidelines:

1. Consult a Professional: Always seek advice from a qualified homeopath or practitioner of gemmotherapy. They can provide tailored recommendations based on the child's symptoms and overall health.

2. Monitor Progress: Keep a close eye on the child's response to the treatments. While natural remedies are generally safe, individual reactions can vary.

3. Integrate with Conventional Medicine: Use homeopathy and gemmotherapy as

complementary therapies. They can be integrated with conventional treatments to enhance overall health and well-being.

By integrating these natural treatments into a child's healthcare routine, parents can support their children's health holistically and gently. Ensure that any new treatment is discussed with a healthcare provider to guarantee safety and effectiveness. By following these tips and offering your child appropriate care, you can help promote healing after head trauma.

Part Four

Coherent Text on Home Remedies and Professional Medical Treatment

CHAPTER 9

A Balanced Approach to Healing: How Home Remedies Helped My Daughter Christella

Treating illnesses is a significant concern and debate among parents and caregivers in childcare. While some advocate for home remedies, others emphasize the importance of professional medical care. This section comprehensively overviews various perspectives on home remedies versus professional medical treatment for children's illnesses. By examining individual experiences and expert opinions, we will explore the benefits and risks associated with both approaches, ultimately offering a balanced view to help parents make informed decisions.

Home remedies, despite their popularity, often lack scientific validation. One contributor highlights the potential dangers of relying solely on these unproven methods. Growing up with frequent illnesses due to a lack of vaccinations and dependence on home remedies, they experienced significant health improvement only after switching to professional medical treatments. This personal testimony underscores the risks of delaying proper medical care, emphasising the need for caution and thorough research before using home remedies. Consulting a general practitioner (GP) when conditions do not improve is crucial to avoid severe health consequences. Another perspective acknowledges that some doctors are well-informed about evidence-based home remedies. These remedies, particularly those derived from plants, can be effective when properly standardised and free from contaminants. However, the lack of regulation in herbal stores poses a significant risk, especially for children, who are more vulnerable to poisoning. This viewpoint stresses the importance of consulting knowledgeable medical professionals and ensuring home remedies are safe and standardised. It also highlights the need to differentiate between minor ailments and serious illnesses that require professional intervention.

The Role of Homeopathy

Homeopathy, a popular alternative medicine, has its proponents and detractors. Homeopathic remedies might offer some relief for minor illnesses like colds without causing harm. However, for severe conditions, they are not a viable substitute for professional medical care. This perspective urges parents to consult doctors for significant diseases, as homeopathy is ineffective. The consensus is that while homeopathy can be part of a holistic approach to minor health issues, it should never replace conventional medical treatment of severe illnesses.

A healthy diet is crucial to a child's ability to fight illnesses. Emphasising home-cooked meals and avoiding processed foods, one parent advocates for a balanced diet rich in nutrients to bolster children's health. They caution against using home remedies without proper medical consultation, highlighting the need for professional care. This approach aligns with the consensus that good nutrition is foundational to health, but it should complement, not replace, professional medical advice and treatment. Many parents rely on their instincts and the advice of paediatric nurses when dealing with common childhood illnesses. One parent shares their strategy of consulting nurses about prevalent diseases and treating symptoms at home unless complications arise. They emphasize the importance of monitoring symptoms, exceptionally high fevers, and trusting parental instincts. This perspective encourages parents to stay informed about common illnesses and seek professional guidance when necessary, balancing home care with medical consultation.

Practical Strategies for Administering Medicine

Understanding the type of illness is crucial before considering home remedies. Visiting a doctor to diagnose the condition ensures that parents make informed treatment decisions. This approach advocates for a preliminary medical consultation to understand the illness, followed by appropriate steps that may include home remedies, provided they are safe and suitable for the child's condition. Specific home remedies can relieve minor ailments like headaches and fevers. Adequate rest, hydration, and cool compresses are some standard methods. However, it is essential to consult a paediatrician before administering any medication or home remedy to ensure safety and proper dosing. Persistent or worsening symptoms should prompt immediate medical attention. This balanced approach emphasizes the importance of professional guidance even when considering seemingly harmless home remedies.

Administering medicine to children can be challenging. One parent shares techniques to make this process less stressful, such as mixing medicine with food or using a reward system. They highlight the importance of making medicine intake a positive experience for the child. In some cases, forceful administration may be necessary for the child's well-being despite the emotional difficulty for parents. This perspective underscores the importance of ensuring children receive essential medications, even if unconventional methods are required. Home remedies are deeply rooted in cultural traditions and familial practices. These remedies, passed down through generations, often rely on natural ingredients available at home. While they can offer comfort and symptom relief for minor ailments, their efficacy is frequently questioned due to insufficient scientific validation. Critics argue that relying on unproven methods can delay necessary medical treatment and potentially worsen the condition. However, there are instances where home remedies, when used cautiously and in conjunction with professional advice, have proven beneficial.

A Personal Experience: Christella's Journey

My daughter Christella's experience serves as a testament to the nuanced effectiveness of home remedies. Christella, a vibrant and active child, began to experience recurrent bouts of a respiratory illness that left her weak and frequently absent from school. Traditional medical treatments provided some relief, but her condition persisted, leading us to explore additional options. We initially followed the conventional route, consulting paediatricians and specialists who prescribed various medications, including antibiotics and inhalers. While these treatments offered temporary relief, they did not completely eradicate the symptoms. Christella's repeated illnesses became a source of concern and frustration for our family. Despite the best efforts of her doctors, it seemed like there was always another episode around the corner. In our quest for a solution, we cautiously incorporated home remedies alongside the prescribed treatments. This decision was not made lightly. We conducted extensive research, consulted with healthcare professionals, and ensured that our chosen remedies were safe and non-invasive. Our primary goal was to complement Christella's medical treatments without replacing them.

One of our first steps was to focus on Christella's diet. Nutrition is crucial in boosting the immune system and promoting overall health. We introduced a diet rich in fruits, vegetables, and whole grains, avoiding processed foods and sugary snacks. Foods like lentils, green vegetables, and nuts became staples in her meals. We also ensured she stayed hydrated and got enough rest.

Natural Remedies and Their Impact

We incorporated specific home remedies known for their respiratory benefits. Honey and ginger tea became a regular part of Christella's routine. Honey has antibacterial properties and can soothe the throat, while ginger is known for its anti-inflammatory effects. We also used steam inhalation with eucalyptus oil to help clear her nasal passages and ease breathing difficulties. These remedies, used in moderation and with careful supervision, began to show positive effects. Throughout this period, we maintained close communication with Christella's paediatrician. Regular check-ups ensured that her condition was monitored professionally and that the home remedies were not interfering with her prescribed treatments. This integrative approach required constant vigilance and a willingness to adjust based on Christella's response to the treatments.

Over time, we observed a noticeable improvement in Christella's health. The frequency and severity of her respiratory episodes decreased significantly. While the home remedies did not cure her condition entirely, they provided additional support that complemented her medical treatments. Christella's overall well-being improved, and she could return to her normal activities more consistently.

Lessons Learned

Christella's journey taught us valuable lessons about the balance between home remedies and professional medical care. Here are some key takeaways:

1. Consultation and Research: Before introducing home remedies, thorough research and professional consultation are essential. This ensures that the remedies are safe and appropriate for the specific condition.

2. Complement, Don't Replace: Home remedies should complement medical treatments, not replace them. Professional medical care remains crucial, especially for severe conditions.

3. Monitoring and Flexibility: Regular monitoring by healthcare professionals is vital to ensure that the condition is managed effectively. Be prepared to adjust the approach based on the child's response.

4. Holistic Health: A holistic approach that includes proper nutrition, rest, and hydration can significantly impact a child's overall health and ability to recover from illnesses.

To conclude, the debate between home remedies and professional medical treatment for children's illnesses highlights the importance of a balanced approach. While home remedies can offer relief and support for minor ailments, they must be used cautiously and with professional medical advice. Christella's journey demonstrates that when used responsibly, home remedies can enhance the effectiveness of conventional treatments and contribute to a child's overall well-being. Parents are encouraged to stay informed, consult healthcare professionals, and trust their instincts while deciding about their child's health. The ultimate goal is to ensure the child's well-being, balancing caution with the necessity of professional medical intervention. By adopting a holistic and integrative approach, parents can provide their children with the best care, ensuring their health and happiness.

Caring for Christella When She Was Sick

When Christella fell ill, it was crucial to ensure she was well taken care of to aid her recovery and provide comfort. Balancing her care while managing other responsibilities required careful planning and attention. Christella had less energy than usual and tired quickly, so I prepared various quiet games to keep her entertained without exhausting her. We played the doctor game, where she pretended to treat me, which made her feel involved and distracted her from her discomfort. Classic board games were also a hit, and I switched up activities regularly to keep her engaged and comfortable. To provide a soothing distraction, we spent time reading together. I chose storybooks and comics that she enjoyed, and we also listened to audiobooks when she was too tired to focus on reading. This helped her rest while keeping her mind off her illness. Christella loved picture books, and we often discussed the images, which kept her entertained and relaxed.

Art activities became a regular part of our routine. I provided Christella with paper, markers, and crayons; she spent hours drawing. She particularly enjoyed creating drawings for her parents, which made her feel appreciated and productive. Sometimes, we printed illustrations from the internet for her to colour, which added variety and excitement to her day.

I made a conscious effort to limit Christella's screen time. While it was tempting to let her watch TV or play on a smartphone, I knew it wouldn't aid her recovery and might make her more anxious. Instead, we focused on other, more beneficial activities for her well-being. It was essential to maintain this balance and not give in to all her demands, teaching her that being sick didn't mean she could have everything she wanted. Keeping Christella hydrated was a top priority. I always had a glass of water nearby, reminding her to drink regularly. We avoided sugary drinks to ensure her digestion wasn't strained. Light and healthy meals were prepared to nourish her and aid her recovery. I ensured her meals were easy to digest, which helped maintain her strength and comfort. Christella's room was kept spotless to prevent the spread of germs and provide a clean environment. I encouraged her to wash her hands frequently and ensured she didn't walk barefoot. For protection, I washed my hands often, wore a mask when necessary, and avoided physical contact as much as possible. Gloves were used during cleaning to prevent the spread of illness further. Throughout her illness, we made sure Christella stayed well-hydrated to prevent dehydration. Light clothing helped her regulate her body temperature naturally. It was important not to give her a cooling bath or use cold compresses and to follow medical advice to avoid these practices.

Christella's illness affected her ability to play with friends and attend school, which was challenging for her. To mitigate these impacts, we focused on activities she enjoyed and could do at home. Her parents made sure to spend quality time with her, balancing attention with her siblings to ensure no one felt neglected. They also sought support and information from healthcare professionals, ensuring they were well-informed and prepared to care for her effectively.

Caring for Christella while sick required a comprehensive approach, balancing medical care, emotional support, and practical strategies. By providing a clean environment, engaging activities, and a healthy diet, we ensured she was comfortable and on the path to recovery. Clear communication with her parents and following professional medical advice were vital components in managing her illness effectively.

Creating a Family Far from Home: The Journey of Christella

Living far from one's homeland and loved ones is a multifaceted experience of challenges and rewards. This journey has been particularly significant for my daughter Christella, shaping her identity and sense of belonging. As her parent, I have experienced first-hand the complexities of creating a family away from my native country and family and how we've formed a new support system in a foreign land.

Leaving the Dominican Republic of the Congo (DRC) was a bittersweet decision. The excitement of starting a new adventure was intertwined with the sorrow of departing from friends and family. The final days in Congo were the most painful, filled with farewells and uncertainties. As we settled, the challenge was about acclimating to a new country and maintaining connections with our loved ones back home. Regular video calls became our lifeline, bridging the distance and keeping relationships alive despite the miles apart. Time seemed to fly, and each reunion with family was a stark reminder of how quickly life changes. The aging of my parents, seen after long separations, was a poignant reminder of the relentless march of time.

Growing up away from her grandparents and extended family in France has been a unique experience for Christella. The language barrier with her grandmother, who speaks only French and our traditional dialect, has been particularly challenging. Christella, fluent only in English, often relies on my wife and me to interpret their conversations. These exchanges sometimes feel like two people speaking different languages, struggling to connect. Despite this, we strive to maintain a bond between them, emphasizing the importance of family ties even across linguistic divides. Living in a foreign country has also given Christella a sense of independence and a broader worldview. The exposure to different cultures and ways of life has enriched her experiences and helped her develop a more inclusive perspective. While she sometimes misses the close-knit family gatherings in DRC, she has learned to appreciate the diverse and multicultural environment she is growing up in.

In our new country, we have been fortunate to build a supportive network that feels like an extended family. Friends and neighbours have stepped into roles that our family members would have filled, offering companionship, support, and a sense of community. This new family has been instrumental in helping us navigate the challenges of expatriate life. Celebrating holidays and special occasions with them has created a sense of belonging and mitigated the loneliness of being away from our homeland. I remember my 35th anniversary. I had a great day in Wimpy with my mum Arlene in South Africa, and I spent 38 years with Julia, Mr Neil's wife.

Creating a new family far from home also involves embracing local traditions and customs. We have consciously immersed ourselves in the local culture, celebrating festivals, learning the language, and participating in community activities. This helps us integrate better and enriches our lives with new experiences and perspectives. Living abroad has its share of joys and challenges. On the one hand, it offers the opportunity to explore new places, meet new people, and experience life from a different vantage point. The excitement of discovering new landscapes, trying new cuisines, and understanding different cultural practices is immensely rewarding. On the other hand, it involves missing essential moments in the lives of our loved ones. Birthdays, anniversaries, and family gatherings are often celebrated through screens, which can be a source of sadness and longing.

For Christella, these dualities are part of her everyday life. She has learned to balance her identity as a child of expatriates with her experiences in the new country. The distance from her extended family has taught her the value of relationships and the importance of staying connected. She has also grown to appreciate the unique blend of cultures that her life embodies. One of the most challenging aspects of living far from home is the guilt of leaving aging parents and family members behind. My parents had envisioned a different life for me, one that involved staying close to home and pursuing a career in France. However, their unwavering support and understanding have been a source of strength for me. They have accepted my choices and continue encouraging me to pursue what makes me happy, even if it means being far away.

For Christella, this experience has underscored the importance of family support and the sacrifices that come with following one's dreams. She has witnessed the complexities of balancing personal aspirations with familial responsibilities and has learned the significance of empathy and understanding in maintaining relationships.

Living far from home is a transformative experience that reshapes one's outlook on life. It involves constantly negotiating between the old and the new, maintaining ties with the past, and embracing the present opportunities. For Christella, this journey has been a lesson in resilience, adaptability, and the importance of community. Despite the challenges, we have created a fulfilling life in our new country. Our experiences have enriched our lives, broadened our horizons, and strengthened our bonds as a family. The support of our new family in this foreign land has been invaluable, providing a sense of belonging and continuity. As we move forward, we continue to cherish our connections with loved ones in my country while embracing the opportunities and relationships in our new home. This duality is a defining aspect of her identity for Christella, offering her a unique perspective on life and relationships.

Creating a family far from one's homeland is a journey of challenges and rewards. It requires resilience, adaptability, and building new connections while maintaining old ones. For Christella, this journey has shaped her into a well-rounded individual with a deep appreciation for both her heritage and the new experiences that life abroad offers. Our story is a testament to the strength of family bonds, the importance of community, and the enriching experience of living in a diverse and multicultural environment.

CHAPTER 10

Towards a Bright Future

Despite our challenges and difficulties along our journey, my family and I have always held onto hope for a better future. Each challenge overcome, each victory won against illness, strengthened our determination to provide our daughter with a safe, loving, and nurturing environment. Beyond the challenges of parenthood lies an infinite love, a force that guides and inspires us in every moment of our family life. Through the ups and downs of our journey, we've learned that parenthood is an endless adventure filled with challenges and, joys, tears, and laughter. But it's also a source of personal growth, deep connection with our children, and gratitude for life's tiny miracles. And it's in this gratitude that we find the strength to keep moving forward, to face challenges with courage and determination, and to embrace each moment with love and compassion.

Every day was a new lesson, an opportunity to grow and evolve as parents. We learned to be patient, flexible, and open to the unexpected. We learned to trust our parental instincts, to listen to our hearts, and to follow our intuition. Through it all, we discovered an inner strength we didn't know we possessed, which enabled us to overcome the most challenging moments with grace and resilience. We also learned the importance of connection and communication in parenthood. We learned to listen to our children, to understand their needs and desires, even when they couldn't express them in words. We learned to be present, attentive, and there for our children in good times and bad. And through this deep connection, we discovered a wealth of family bonds that nourished and supported us throughout our journey.

But above all, we learned that love is the key to everything. Love for our children, for our family, for ourselves. Love strengthens us and helps us keep moving forward, even when times are tough. Love unites us, guides us, and inspires us to be the best possible parents for our children. And it's in this infinite love that we find our greatest strength and joy as a family. In every trial and moment of doubt, we drew upon our unconditional love for our daughter and family to find the strength to keep moving forward. This love was our anchor, our rock, holding us firmly when the waves of adversity threatened to sweep us away. It was our light in the darkness, our guide in the storm, showing us the way to a brighter, more hopeful future. We've weathered storms and trials together, but we've always found refuge in our mutual love and commitment to our family. Every obstacle overcome was a victory for us all, a testament to our resilience and determination to overcome whatever challenges lay in our path. And through it all, we've grown together as a family, as human beings, drawing upon our love to rise above adversity and become stronger together.

Today, as we look back on our journey with gratitude and humility, we've traversed dark valleys and dazzling peaks, but at every step, we've been guided by our love for each other. And as we continue to move forward into the future, we know that no matter what life may bring, we'll face it together with love, courage, and determination. For at the heart of everything we do, there is love. Love that unites us, supports us and gives us the strength to overcome any challenge. And it's in this love that we find our greatest strength, joy, and tremendous gratitude for the wonders of parenthood and family life. Thus, whatever the future holds in store for us, we know we'll face it with love, courage, and determination. For as long as we have our love for each other, we'll have everything we need to overcome anything, triumph over anything, and live every moment with gratitude and joyfully. I genuinely hope any new parent (or reader) who finds this book has learned something from my family's journey. I wish that you take at least one thing from this tumultuous journey of parenthood and that this book brings comfort, laughter, and strength to all going through similar trials.

References

1. "The Happiest Baby on the Block" par Harvey Karp; 2015. Ed: Bantam Books

2. "Caring for Your Baby and Young Child: Birth to Age 5" de l'American Academy of Pediatrics; 2019 ed: Bantam Books

3. "Mayo Clinic Guide to Your Baby's First Year" de Mayo Clinic, 2012. Mayo Clinic Press

4. "Healthy Sleep Habits, Happy Child" par Marc Weissbluth, 2003 Ballantine Books

5. "The Wonder Weeks" par Frans X. Plooij, 2017. Kiddy World Publishing

6. "The Vaccine-Friendly Plan: Dr. Paul's Safe and Effective Approach to Immunity and Health—from Pregnancy Through Your Child's Teen Years" par Paul Thomas et Jennifer Margulis. Ed. Ballantine Books

7. "The Baby Book: Everything You Need to Know About Your Baby from Birth to Age Two" par William Sears et Martha Sears, 2013. Little, Brown and Company

8. "Parenting with Love and Logic: Teaching Children Responsibility" par Foster Cline et Jim Fay 2006. Ed. NavPress

9. "The Whole-Brain Child: 12 Revolutionary Strategies to Nurture Your Child's Developing Mind" par Daniel J. Siegel et Tina Payne Bryson. 2011. Éd, Bantam Books

10. "The Womanly Art of Breastfeeding" par Diane Wiessinger, Diana West et Teresa Pitman 2010, Éd. Ballantine Books

11. (4) Musso P, Chiappini E, Bernardini R. Human Microbiome and Allergic Diseases in 16(2):89-94. doi: 10.2174/1573396315666191025110849. PMID: 31654515.

12. (8) Kloepfer KM, Kennedy JL. Childhood respiratory viral infections and the microbiome. J Allergy Clin Immunol. 2023 Oct;152(4):827-834. doi: 10.1016/j.jaci.2023.08.008. Epub 2023 Aug 20. PMCID: PMC10592030.

13. Nițu, S., 2015. THE EFFECTIVENESS OF GEMMOTHERAPY IN CURRENT MEDICAL PRACTICE. *Jurnal Medical Aradean (Arad Medical Journal)*, *18*(1), pp.72-74.

14. Raiciu, A.D., 2019, October. Gemmotherapy—Modern Medicine. In *Proceedings* (Vol. 29, No. 1, p. 117). MDPI.

15. Trapani, D.G., 2013. Revue Internationale sur le Médicament, vol. 5 (1), 2013. *Revue Internationale sur le Médicament*, *5*(1), p.47.

www.ingramcontent.com/pod-product-compliance
Lightning Source LLC
LaVergne TN
LVHW011207080426
835508LV00007B/639